MIDLIFE
MEDITATIONS

by
Chuck Anderson

PublishAmerica
Baltimore

First printing

PublishAmerica has allowed this work to remain exactly as the author intended, verbatim, without editorial input.

Hardcover 978-1-4626-3040-0
Softcover 978-1-4626-3041-7
PUBLISHED BY PUBLISHAMERICA, LLLP
www.publishamerica.com
Baltimore

Printed in the United States of America

This book is dedicated to my sons, who taught me how to be a father.

I would like to acknowledge the various editors with whom I have worked for many years: Kevin Molloy, Jeff Sievers, and Frank Costanza. Their advice and encouragement has been invaluable.

Foreword

For over ten years, the author worked as a reporter and occasional editor for a couple of weekly newspapers. During that time, he not only covered the news, but also was given the opportunity to express himself in a series of opinion/editorial pieces, known in the trade as "OP/ED." In the tradition of Montaigne, Charles Lamb, and Ralph Waldo Emerson, though in no way as profound, the author wrote essays about life, love, and everyday subjects like home maintenance, marriage, and buying a car. The art of the essay is alive and thriving, as such writing is still found in such magazines as *Time*, *Newsweek*, *The Saturday Review*, even in blogs on the Internet.

The author is grateful to the publisher of the Long Island Advance and the Suffolk County News, John Tuthill III, for his permission to reprint most of the pieces in this book.

TABLE OF CONTENTS

About Buddy

Recently we went to see a movie called "Simon Birch," a sentimental tale about the friendship of two boys, one of whom was a congenital dwarf who believed that God had a purpose for him.

The movie was derived from *A Prayer for Owen Meany* by John Irving, his finest book since *The World According to Garp,* in my estimation.

Simon Birch reminded me of a long ago friend whose name was Buddy.

When Buddy and his family first moved to our neighborhood, my mother did her Welcome Wagon thing: take a cake over and find out what the new neighbors were like. She came home and announced that she had offered my services as a playmate-companion to Buddy, whom she described as "kind of different."

The next day, this reluctant volunteer trudged across the street and rang the bell. I was greeted at the door by Buddy's sister Annabelle, who was to become the first love of my life, and ushered into a room where everything was at floor level.

There sat Buddy, a fifteen-year-old with a normal-sized head and the body of a baby. He was wearing a tiny cowboy hat and vest, with a brace of toy cap pistols at his belt. An interest in the West turned out to be one of the things we had in common, as I was going through a Zane Grey phase at the time. In the weeks and months to come, Buddy and I would spend many hours listening to "The Lone Ranger" on the radio, and he would come to refer to me as "Tonto." Buddy may have been trapped inside his deformed body, but his spirit roamed the great plains.

We had other mutual interests: the New York Giants, checkers, and his sister Annabelle. He conned me out of my best baseball cards, beat me regularly at checkers, and introduced me to chess. Before I left after each visit, Annabelle and I would sneak a chaste kiss in the front hall, an event that took the sting out of losing at checkers.

I will never forget Buddy's laugh, a deep chortle that bubbled out of his tiny body as he took my last piece with a short, deformed little hand. He laughed a lot: at me, at himself, at his sister, at the world at large.

In the changing voice of an adolescent, Buddy would tease me about his sister, about my size and early teenage clumsiness, about my inability to play checkers and chess.

This was well before the days of special education, so Buddy had a tutor. Had the family been less well off, he probably would have been shut up in some kind of special institution. Nevertheless, he was eager to find out what went on in school every day, and would press me for details: what the teachers and the other children were like, what went on in the playground, what we had for lunch.

Nowadays, the buzz word in special education is "inclusion," which means that students like Buddy would be in an electrically-operated wheelchair, sitting in as many regular classrooms as possible. What a wonderful addition he would have made to any of my classes, had we known any better. All I knew at the time was that this was my first experience with someone who was, as we say today, "physically challenged."

Our friendship lasted for about a year. When I returned from a summer of working as a camp counselor in Maine, I found that Buddy and his family had moved away. His father was a chemist for Pfizer, and was re-assigned to a plant in South America or some such far-flung place.

Later, we learned that Buddy had died. We never found out how or why, but that doesn't seem to be important.

It's how he lived that counts.

Back to School

This fall, I am going back to school for the 66th year. Maybe I'll get it right this time.

As a lefty, I remember having difficulty learning how to write in elementary school. Steel-tipped pens were not developed for left-handers. As I struggled with Latin and algebra in the ninth grade, I dreaded the idea of going to high school. I never thought I would make it through high school, go on to college.

As an educator who has worked for 50 years, I am used to following the academic calendar. For me, the year starts in September, not January, and ends in June. Don't ask me about summer. That has always been a time for part-time summer jobs to support a growing family, and when the boys grew up and left the nest, a time for long-delayed travel.

(The following piece was published a few years ago.)

Sometimes when you're a teacher, going back to school in the fall reminds you that you're getting old. Consider this year's incoming college freshmen.

The youngsters starting college this fall were mostly born in 1981. That means they have no meaningful recollection of the Reagan years, nor do they know that he had been shot. Moreover, they were pre-teenagers when the Persian Gulf War took place.

They were age eleven when the Soviet Union broke up, and do not remember much about the Cold War. They think that the notion of bomb shelters in the backyard is pre-historic. They have never feared a nuclear war. "The Day After" is a pill to them, not a movie.

Most of them are too young to remember the space shuttle blowing up. In terms of economics, Black Monday of 1987 is about as significant to them as the Great Depression.

They have never had a polio shot, and do not know what it is. However, their lifetime has always included AIDS.

Bottle caps have not only always been the kind that screws off, but have always been plastic.

Vinyl record albums are things of the ancient past to them, they have never owned a record player, and the expression "You sound like a broken record" means nothing. They may have heard of an eight-track, but chances are they have never seen or heard one. The compact disc was introduced when they were two years old. They were born the year after Walkman was introduced by SONY.

The early "Star Wars" films look fake to them, and they feel the special effects are pathetic.

As far as they are concerned, there have always been red M&M's, and blue ones are nothing new. What do you mean there used to be beige ones?

As far as they know, stamps have always cost about 33 cents, and they have always had a telephone answering machine.

Most have never seen a television set with only 13 channels, nor have they seen a black and white TV. They have always had cable, and there have always been VCR's. They cannot fathom what it's like to watch TV without a remote control.

Roller skating has always meant in-line for them.

To them, Jay Leno has always been the host of the "Tonight Show." They don't know who Mork was, or where he was from. They do not care who shot J.R., and have no idea who J.R. is. They have never heard the terms: "Where's the beef?" "I'd walk a mile for a Camel" or "De plane! De plane!"

They have never seen Larry Bird or Kareem Abdul-Jabbar play. They never took a swim and thought about "Jaws," or took a shower and thought about "Psycho."

To them, the Viet Nam War is ancient history, and they have no idea that Americans were ever held hostage in Iran.

There has always been MTV and CNN, and popcorn has always been cooked in a microwave.

Are we getting old, or what?

A Meditation on Home Repair

One thing my father never told me about buying a house is that I would be destined to spend the rest of my life repairing it. Very few people bought new houses back in the early sixties. I'm not sure, but there may have been not much of a market at the time. At any rate, we bought a house that was about 20 years old, beginning my never-ending odyssey in home repair.

In the last 40 years, we have put two new roofs over the original, added two extensions to accommodate our growing family, painted the exterior of the house twice, and built a deck, a tool shed, and a gazebo. I get tired just thinking about these projects. Since I was a school teacher at the time, these major home improvements were undertaken during the summer months, not the most ideal time to be re-shingling a roof, I will admit.

If we ever put another roof on the house, we will have to rip off the first three. I think I will leave that chore for the next owner.

We had to tear down the tool shed and the gazebo, I'm sorry to say. Last year we decided to set our house in order in case we wanted to sell it and move to a sybaritic condominium in Florida. The Town Building Department informed us that we needed Certificates of Occupancy for the deck, the gazebo, one of the additions, and the tool shed. I could not understand why we needed a CO for the shed. Maybe it was for the hornets who nested under the roof. Also, I could not fathom why we needed a Certificate of Occupancy for something we had already occupied for 20 years. Moreover, it turned out that we needed something called a "variance," costing hundreds of dollars and a hearing before the Planning Board, to keep the shed and the gazebo, so they had to come down.

We don't need the extensions anymore; our family has shrunken to two since our boys moved out. But I have decided to paint most of the house again, and put natural shingles on the front. Of course, I chose a week that saw record-breaking heat to begin this latest madness.

I have often wondered what it is that drives us to take up hammer and saw in the hottest months of the year. Is it the smell of freshly cut wood in the morning, or the satisfying feel of driving a nail home in two strokes? I suspect that it might have something to do with leading a sedentary life, pushing paper most of the year. It is a refreshing change to work with one's hands for a couple of weeks, embracing the cuts and scratches, the sore knees and aching back.

Or maybe I'm just a glutton for punishment.

The Great Homework Debate

There was a time when everybody did homework. It was a necessary routine, like brushing your teeth before you went to bed. It was part of the American way, a Horatio Alger thing.

Sure, in every high school there was a duck-tailed leather jacket who remained defiant to the bitter end and dropped out at age 16 to work in the local garage. But for the most part, homework was what you did if you went to school.

Thirty years ago, it was generally believed that at least a half an hour of homework for each major subject would be sufficient. Then came television, and the easy years, when the only people doing homework were the nerds who aimed for Harvard and Caltech. In the free fall Seventies, a commonly held belief among adolescents was that homework made you ugly.

That may be why more and more colleges and universities found themselves scheduling remedial courses in math and composition. Some local community colleges even had to schedule pre-remedial courses.

Up until recently, a few high schools in the area had an unofficial, unspoken policy: "Don't assign any homework to the general students. They won't do it anyway."

Lately there has been a sea change in education, brought about by the new Regents mandate in New York, and the No Child Left Behind philosophy from Washington. Educators are running scared, and one way they are dealing with the problem is to assign massive amounts of homework.

Now students are getting an hour's worth of homework per subject, and they are overwhelmed, as are their teachers, who have to look at all the stuff. Imagine that you are an English teacher with 135 students (the norm in this area). You assign one paper a week to these students. To do the job right, it will take you about eight hours a week to evaluate and grade those papers. Whether assigning lots of homework will prepare students for the new Regents remains to be seen, but it's a step in the right direction.

As we enter the new budget cycle for next year, local educators and school trustees will be wrestling with a whole new set of priorities: how to get students ready for the universal Regents exams. Some districts, such as ours, see a technology initiative and the purchase of new computers as the answer to the problem. In addition to our district, other school systems are looking at extended early childhood education and the addition of a summer school program as well.

In the final analysis, preparing for the new Regents examinations will be costly. While there is some state aid to offset the additional expense, local taxpayers should be prepared to dig a little deeper into their pockets to pay for increased school taxes.

They may have to make some tough decisions, like cutting back on such electives as "Marriage and the Family" and "Wild Birds of Long Island," to pay for enhanced academics.

And before the taxpayers vote on the budget, they had better do some homework themselves.

The Stop Sign Wars

A war has begun in our little village. It is not a global catastrophe, and will not require the services of the United Nations. However minor it may seem in the larger scheme of things, this conflict represents the struggle between the forces of darkness and those who advocate law and order, and therefore it needs to be noted for posterity.

A few weeks ago, on a remote intersection of our sleepy little community, there appeared three stop signs, planted by elves in the night, it seemed. They were suddenly just there, three red octagons shouting their warning against a background of muted browns and greens of the National Wildlife Refuge that runs along the east side of a nearby road.

They appeared so suddenly that we, and evidently many drivers, did not notice them at first. For the first couple of days, there was the sound of rubber on asphalt as brakes were applied too late, followed by the angry roar of acceleration. This particular section is scantily populated, bordered on one side by the refuge and on the other by a large tract recently acquired by a local foundation dedicated to open space. It is a straightaway where, if one is so inclined, high speed driving may be practiced, if the driver is not worried about hitting a deer or an occasional child.

In the neighborhood, there are conflicting stories as to the origin of the signs. A fellow up the street said he was at a school concert with the town supervisor, and expressed his concern over racing vehicles on a road where several school bus stops are located.

We met another neighbor walking her dog, and she said that her husband, a doctor treating the supervisor's mother-in-law, had been asked what he wanted in return, besides his fee, one presumes. The doctor, who lives on the corner in question, purportedly asked for the sign placement.

One or both stories are probably true, and our town supervisor, who has gained a reputation for being responsive to the needs of his constituents, obviously took appropriate action. The response from the neighborhood has been positive, as there are a number of young children on our street who wait at the bus stop at the intersection.

One or two nights after the signs went up, the wars began. Walking our dog in the morning, we found that two of the sentinels had been rudely pulled from the ground and left lying on their side like wounded soldiers.

The next day, they were back on duty, restored to their rightful position by vigilant highway workers.

A few days passed, then one of the signs disappeared altogether, and the other was found in the woods, ignominiously dumped on its head. The battle had been enjoined.

We called the highway department, who referred us to the department of public safety, who referred us to…well, you know how it goes. When we finally reached the person in charge of sign restoration, he said, "We'll get right on it." As if to verify his claim of speedy service, we heard him speak to his troops on what appeared to be a short wave transmitter. It turned out that they were waiting for orders at the local delicatessen just around the corner, as was their custom. They would be on their way to the scene, just as soon as they finished their coffee and donuts.

During our call, we asked the person in charge of sign restoration why they didn't sink the signs in a concrete base. He said, "Can't do that. It's against regulations. What if someone hits the sign?" We had a mental image of a disgruntled speeder attacking the sign with his car.

The next morning, we found that the anti-sign forces had tried another strategy: a black arrow had been spray-painted on the face of the southbound sign, with the word "Go!"

Lately, we have noticed that the drivers who go north and south on the road have been observing the signs, reluctantly rolling to a stop, pausing, then going ahead.

It would appear that a truce has been declared.

On Ghosts

Halloween is almost upon us, and shortly thereafter is an off-year election, so it seems to be a good time to talk about ghosts and things that go bump in the night.

We're not talking about some local politicians we know, who do not seem to have a ghost of a chance in the local elections, or are we talking about eggs hitting the side of our house or some demented hooligan deriving pleasure by smashing mailboxes up and down the street.

First, there seems to be a plethora of ghost movies on television and at the movies, reminding us that there are spirits abroad. From "The Ghost and Mrs. Muir" to "Ghostbusters" to "Casper the Friendly Ghost," these films are part of our common cultural heritage.

Spirits figured prominently in early Roman drama, and everyone knows about the Ghost in *Hamlet*, a character, it is said, that Shakespeare himself liked to play on occasion. There is *Ghosts,* a play by Henrik Ibsen, about the haunting malice of nature in transmitting evil traits by heredity, where the sins of the father are visited on the son.

It may sound like heresy for an English professor to say this, but the problem with films and plays is that when it comes to ghosts, they don't leave much to the imagination. Since an appreciation of ghosts is based the fears that dwell in our fancy, there is nothing like a good book or ghost story well told to raise the hackles on the back of our necks.

The first and one of the best ghost stories I ever read was "The Legend of Sleepy Hollow," by Washington Irving. The story of Ichabod Crane and his night flight from the Headless

Horseman is a classic, and deserves re-reading or re-telling at this time of year.

For youngsters, there is Jane Yolen's *Here There Be Ghosts,* a book of stories and poems about specters, the dead and the undead, hallucinations of the mind, and emanations of the soul. For older readers, what better time to revisit "The Tell-Tale Heart" or "The Black Cat" by Edgar Allan Poe, or the New Yorker collection of the cartoons of Charles Addams, a compendium of ghoulish hilarity?

For those who claim to be interested in "real" ghosts, there is an organization made up of normal people who happen to have an above-average interest in paranormal phenomena.

These are the kind of people who would take down accounts of Hitchhiking Hattie, an apparition who has been haunting the highways and byways of New York State since her first appearance up near Albany in 1920.

It seems that a man had been to a party out in the country near Albany. About midnight, he was on his way home in a heavy downpour. Passing Graceland Cemetery, he saw a young girl in a white dress. Though she did not signal to him, he had the feeling that she wanted a ride. Since the passenger side door of his coupe was jammed, he got out and let her slide over under the wheel to her side of the car. They didn't talk much, because the rain was coming down so hard he had to concentrate on his driving. The girl told him she lived on Lark Street, so he headed for that address. When he pulled up in front of the house, he turned to look at the girl, but she was gone. All that was left was a little puddle of water on the floor. The man went to the house, and a woman in a flannel bathrobe answered the bell. He began to tell her the story, when she interrupted, "You don't need to go on, young man. It's my daughter again. It often happens on rainy nights, that's when she seems to want to come home.

You understand, she's been buried up at Graceland for nearly four years now."

On the web site, www.ghosthunter.org, members of the Society for Paranormal Investigation and Informational Training (SPIRIT) come together and swap tales like the one about Hattie the Hitchhiker, who has appeared and reappeared many times since 1920.

Finally, there are the ghosts who lurk in our psyche, the shades of unrequited loves and failed relationships, the spirits of misdeeds gone unacknowledged and unpunished, such as the high school French teacher upon whose doorstep we left a leaning tombstone as a Halloween prank.

Forgive me, Madame Arnot.

How to Survive in College

A month or so ago, many young people from the area are headed off to college, for the first time or as returning students. They carry with them the hopes, dreams, and fears of doting and proud parents, as well as a hefty financial responsibility, in many cases.

New to the college scene or not, some students find that there are some expectations and realities about college that may come as a rude awakening.

For example, there is the matter of grades. When college students receive their first round of grades, the room is usually filled with shocked gasps and an occasional sob. Students who are used to getting A's and B's (after all, that's how they got into college in the first place) are horrified to find C's and even D's on their papers. What they quickly and painfully realize is that there is a difference in grading standards between high school and college. Most university catalogues point out that a C means that the student has met the requirements of the assignment, no more, no less. An A indicates that the student's academic performance in achieving the objectives of the assignment was of honors level; a B shows that the student's performance in achieving the objectives of the assignment was distinctly above that required by the course; a D shows that the student's performance was less than required by the course, but may be sufficient to receive credit; however, this grade is usually not acceptable in a major or minor course.

Next there is the matter of what to take to college. We recently overheard a young coed exclaim, "After packing all my toys (TV set, stereo, computer, skis, roller blades, etc.), I don't have room for my clothes." When we heard this, several thoughts occurred to us: Was this youngster taking a dictionary or thesaurus, absolutely essential for freshman English? Then we realized we were showing our age, for the computer would no doubt have a built-in dictionary, thesaurus, spell-check, and grammar-check. (Most students forget that a spell check misses homonyms like *too* and *to* or *their* and *they're*.) However, we also wondered if this youngster was going to school to work or play.

Speaking of computers: In spite of advertising and peer pressure, students do not need to purchase a computer to succeed in college. Most schools have numerous computer centers available to the students, and in many cases, may lease computers to students for a nominal fee. In many schools, there are computer rooms in the dorms.

Another young man of our acquaintance got outfitted to go to a college in northern New England by purchasing the latest in cold weather apparel from L.L. Bean: lined pants, down jacket, heavy underwear. When he got to school, he found that even in the dead of winter, everyone wore workboots, shorts, and a plaid wool shirt over a T-shirt, and would race from warm and cozy dorm to overheated classroom through foot-high snow.

About professors: Students should not expect full professors in their first couple of years. Chances are students will be taught by graduate assistants, who know absolutely nothing about teaching, or adjuncts, who know a lot about teaching, since many of them are high school retirees.

Many college students have difficulty with the notion that it is their job to please the professor, whatever his rank. Some of the following bits of advice may sound simplistic, but they truly apply at the college level.

First, come to class and do good work. That may sound obvious, but it's true. Only a fool parties during the week and doesn't get up in time for class.

Second, get a good seat. College teachers do not usually use seating charts. The good students always seem to sit in the front rows, and the indifferent or chronically late students wind up in the back.

Next, appear as if you're interested in the class. Look the professor in the eye and ask a relevant question once in awhile. Most instructors love it when you ask a question; it validates their existence. Above all, don't yawn, even if you spent half the night reading the assignment. A surefire way to antagonize a professor is to slouch in with a cap pulled down over your eyes, with no notebook or pen, and hunker down in the back row. You may think you look cool, but most professors are not impressed by this demeanor.

Get to class on time. You may have to wait for the professor, but he won't wait to start without you, and he will consider your late arrival annoying. There is a double standard here, but that's the way it is.

Find out what you can about your professor. At Hofstra University, where the students rate the professors each semester, there is a compilation on each professor and how he stacks up against the rest of the department available in the reference section of the library. In other schools, you may have to rely on word of mouth or look up ratemyprofessor.com.

Visit your professor during his office hours, especially if you are having a problem with the course or an assignment. They are paid to keep office hours, and it is a way for them to know you better. Many colleges have started a mentoring or buddy system to help students make the transition between high school and college. Sadly, not enough students take advantage of these programs.

If you have a learning disability, do not be afraid to reveal it to the appropriate college authorities, who will in turn notify the professor. There's nothing to be ashamed of; after all, Einstein had a learning disability.

Finally, make sure your work is neat and handed in on time. Most professors do not accept late assignments, and turn a deaf ear to just about any excuse you can think up.

Let's face it, Dorothy, you're not in Kansas anymore.

Veteran's Day thoughts

Since yesterday was Veteran's Day, thoughts of those who have served our country are still in our minds.

There were no local parades yesterday, no major consecrations. A modest wreath or two was laid at the Viet Nam Memorial on Bald Hill. As we look at the memorial, we may still harbor angry thoughts about the delinquents who took it upon themselves to twice desecrate with graffiti the memory of the veterans who died in Southeast Asia. We thought of a Kafkaesque but appropriate punishment for these hooligans: tattoo them with every name on the VietNam Wall in Washington, just to remind them whom they have affronted.

Television commentators had a few words about Veteran's Day, as well as newspaper editorial writers, but we don't seem to make a big deal over this occasion any more.

A thought or two may occur to us as we pass the Vet's Place in Yaphank, home for wayward veterans who never got it back together after returning from the jungles of Viet Nam or the deserts of the Near East.

Recently, several media events have returned the veteran to our collective consciousness. First, there was "Saving Private Ryan," the Steven Spielberg film that showed us the horrors of war. After watching the film, we were reminded of a visit to Normandy, to the American and British cemeteries. Among the thousands of white markers, we remember the individuals who were buried there: brother and brother, father and son, father and sons.

Then there is the fine book by Stephen E. Ambrose, *Citizen Soldiers,* which chronicles the war in Europe from D-Day to the Battle of the Bulge, a series of battles fought by ordinary people who could have come from your neighborhood.

Finally, there is "A Soldier's Daughter Never Cries," a respectful, moving film adaptation of Kaylie Jones' semi-autobiographical novel about growing up in the last years of the life of her father, James Jones, who wrote the definitive war novel. These stories remind us that it is not only the veteran who suffers from war, but the veteran's family, and by extension, his country, as well.

So let us once again consecrate Veteran's Day, for what affects the veteran affects us all. As John Donne said, "Send not to know for whom the bell tolls, it tolls for thee."

On the Death of Manners

My family thinks I drive too fast.

That may be so, but, as I explain to them, it is because I am trying to get away from the giant sports utility vehicles that seem to proliferate the highways and byways these days, as they charge up behind me at night with their high beams on, tailgating my car until I pull over and let them pass.

Or it may be to avoid those behemoths of the road, the trash trucks that rocket between the local landfill and a garbage processing plant in the next county. Every time I clock one of them, they are going almost 80 miles an hour. Think of several tons of metal traveling at that speed; a guy in a Honda Civic wouldn't stand a chance. They must be paid by the load, maybe that explains the rush.

A few years ago, I took a defensive driving course, partly at the urging of my nervous family, and partly because I wanted to get a ten percent discount on my insurance bill. During the course, the instructor told us that the correct protocol for highway entrances and exits is to give way to the fellow entering the road in front of us. In other words, if we are entering a highway from a service road or entrance, the motorists already on the road are supposed to practice a sort of vehicular "After you, Alphonse," slow down, and let us get on the highway with impunity.

The notion made sense to us, but every time we tried it, we were nearly run off the road by the oncoming cars, whose drivers clearly had not taken a defensive driving course lately, if ever.

One day, we were trying to exit the highway to go north on another road when a young man, ignoring our right turn directional signal, came roaring up and attempted to pass us on the right, shouldering us out of the exit lane. I shook my "teacher finger" at him, and my companion may have mouthed some imprecation, though I didn't hear anything. He may have mistaken my gesture for one that is more vulgar in the coinage of sign language, or he may have read my passenger's lips and taken offense, for he rolled down his window and began to shout obscentities at us, demanding that I stop the car and prove my manhood or some such thing. This confrontation continued for what seemed like minutes, though I'm sure it was only seconds, before he sped away in high dudgeon.

To many this may sound like an example of what has been described as "road rage;" however, I see it as an example of the slow death of manners in modern civilization.

Take a ride on a local highway during the morning or evening rush hour. Watch the cars speeding up the left turn lane before each light, only to cut in front of every one waiting for the light to change. Observe the cars waiting for a break in the traffic so they can get on the highway. If someone slows down to allow another motorist to get on the highway, he risks a chorus of angry horn blowing from other drivers. Since so many drivers seem to be running red lights lately, we have taken to waiting for a few seconds after our light has turned green before proceeding. Truly, a "me first" attitude seems to prevail on the roads these days.

In the book *All I Really Need to Know I Learned in Kindergarten.* author Robert Fulghum reveals some principles that should follow us for the rest of our days, and some of them apply to our increasingly crowded roads.

Fulghum says, "Share everything," to which we add, "including the road." Another principle: "Don't hit people," (especially with your car or truck.) The list goes on: "Clean up your own mess. (Don't litter.) Don't take things that aren't yours. (Even if someone leaves the keys in the ignition.) Say you're sorry when you hurt somebody. When you go out in the world, watch out for traffic, hold hands, and stick together. Goldfish and hamsters and white mice all die. So do we. (Hopefully, in our beds and not in an automobile accident.) And then remember the Dick and Jane books and the first word you learned, the biggest word of all, "LOOK."

It seems to me that if we followed these principles on the road, with a little Golden Rule thrown in for good measure, we should be able to do something about the decline of good manners on the road. Or maybe I'll just buy a HumVee.

A Few Thoughts on the Day after Thanksgiving

A few years ago, we began a custom that has become more entrenched with time: on the day after Thanksgiving, we drive out east, about as far away from the malls as we can get. One year, we drove to Montauk Point, the end of civilization as we know it. This year, we got as far as Easthampton, and went to the movies with a lot of like-minded folks.

As we looked around, the movie theater seemed to be filled with middle-aged couples, who looked slightly guilty about avoiding what has become a national mania: going shopping the day after Thanksgiving. Silently, we saluted them for their courage and ability to resist the siren song of the massive advertising that permeates the print media and the airwaves.

Let's face it, the pressure to go into debt for the next three or four months is enormous.

It's not that we are Grinches about Christmas and all that. In fact, before we left, we purchased a Furby, this year's hottest toy, for "only $99.95" on the internet. The Furby, described as a "stuffed animal with attitude," is purported to be both snuggly and smart. It is said to speak an imaginary language called Furbish, but eventually learns English and begins to act like a twitchy four-year-old, laughing when tickled and singing jingles on cue. Hey, who needs a puppy for Christmas when you can get a Furby? No more messy newspapers or fleas, just an occasional battery replacement.

Our satisfaction at getting this sought-after toy for our granddaughter was diminished somewhat when we read in the newspaper that they were priced at $30. Gnashing our teeth, headed east, brooding about a brave new world filled with interactive toys and virtual pets instead of games like Candy Land and Monopoly.

There is something about driving to the eastern end of Long Island at this time of year. The summer crowds are gone, and a lot of restaurants and other establishments are beginning to close for the winter. The fall foliage has all but disappeared, and the muted browns, mauves, and grays of winter cover the fields and woods. Everything seems to be done in pastels.

The tension and stress of preparing for Thanksgiving dinner seemed to drop off our shoulders as the miles went by. Long Island seemed to become more like New England as we drove down the Currier and Ives Main Street of Easthampton. We would not have been surprised to see an itinerant Pilgrim looking for a spot of Wild Turkey.

After the movie, we enjoyed a leisurely, candle-lit dinner at Alison's By the Sea, the moment marred only by some raucous yuppies at a nearby table bragging about their sports utility vehicles. Why they needed that kind of transportation to get from Manhatten to the Hamptons escapes me, unless they planned to drive them on the beach, an unlikely activity, considering this bunch, mostly wearing Gucci loafers.

Returning home, we felt somehow refreshed and restored, ready for tree lightings, holiday parades, office parties, and the like. More than anything, we were sustained by a decision reached at dinner: to head south the day after Christmas.

Key West, here we come!

What I Want for Christmas

"All I want for Christmas is my two front teeth," goes the old song, or something to that effect; however, I've reached the age where I am inestimably grateful for any front teeth left to me. At this time of year, as the leaves begin to turn and drift down from the trees and I finally close the pool, I start dropping Christmas gift hints to my family.

I do this in part because I want to help them out, to save them from the conundrum of what to give to someone who doesn't appear to really need anything. I don't have any hobbies to speak of, though in the last couple of years I have taken up hiking and returned to golfing. In the last few Christmases and birthdays, my family has pretty much exhausted the gift possibilities in those areas.

They know I like to read, but since I buy one or two books a week and visit the library with some regularity, they have given up the notion of buying the latest best seller. I will have probably read it by the time Christmas arrives anyway.

So as a service to my family and friends, here is my Christmas wish list for this year, not necessarily in order of preference:

First, I would like to have the new theater in the next town show films that do not appear in the surrounding multiplexes, the kind that we have to drive to Huntington or East Hampton to see, "art films" like "Life is Beautiful" and "Il Postino."

Second, I would like to see one-way streets in and out of the next town. Main Street could be one way going west, and the adjacent streets one way going east. All it would take is a few signs and a little getting used to.

Third, I would like to see a special tax on all sports utility vehicles—the Explorers, the Navigators, the Terminators—that seem to be cluttering up the roads these days. We're paying for these gas guzzlers, when you think about it, because they make the demand for gas go up, and along with it, the price. They also use up more natural resources, and create more wear and tear on the roads we support with our taxes.

In the same vein, I would love to see some kind of speed control built into the ash-for-trash behemoths that barrel from Yaphank to Hempstead and back, so they could not drive more than 55 miles per hour.

Fourth, I would like to see everybody vote in the upcoming elections for the quarter penny sales tax extension, which will eventually go towards protection of our water resources, sewer district rate stabilization, and finish the county's farm and open space protection programs.

Fifth, I would like someone to look into the "franchise fee" on my cablevision bill. My understanding of the fee is that it defrays the cost of the franchise payment made by the cable company to the municipal organization that gives it permission to operate within its boundaries, in this case Brookhaven Town. It's only about $2.50 a month, but when you multiply that amount by the thousands of subscribers in the area, that's a lot of money.

Sixth, I would wish for the Long Island Railroad to mute its horns, especially at night. It would be nice to get a full night's sleep instead of being awakened at 2:00 and 4:00 p.m. with maddening regularity.

Finally, I would wish for a couple of Y2K-free airline tickets to take us to Southern Italy right after Christmas. I guess that's a present I'll have to buy for myself, and keep my fingers crossed that the Alitalia computers are up to speed.

A Dissertation on Calendars

This is the moment of the year when our thoughts invariably turn to calendars, those linear metaphors for time that seem to rule our lives with appointments, deadlines, and due dates.

It all starts when the office manager brings in a new desk calendar, a signal to throw out the ragged, coffee-stained desk covering that represents a year's worth of news stories and telephone calls. This existential wrench is followed by a visit to the bookstore, where we are confronted with the usual plethora of gift calendars, those offerings we make to others when our imagination fails us. With some regret, we force ourselves to discard the Sports Illustrated or Absolut Vodka calendars presented to us last Christmas, with the faint hope that we will get this year's version to replace them. However, we are loathe to part with the bamboo calendar depicting the Year of the Ox, acquired at our favorite Chinese take-out. Perhaps we will leave it on the office wall, as a kind of decorative art.

While most of us are out buying new date books and calendars, those who toil in the academic world are ruled by a different time scheme, for they follow a different time frame: their calendar begins in September, forcing many of them to live in two worlds.

The tax gatherers have their calendar as well, which does not seem to jibe with the rest of the world. It is ironic that their bill arrives just after the two most expensive times for many families: Christmas and graduation.

While Hanukkah started just before Christmas this year, and Kwanzaa is celebrated the week between Christmas and New Year's, we are reminded that different faiths follow different calendars.

The western world begins the year with January, named for the Roman god Janus, whose two-faced image adorned many Latin doorways. Appropriately, he is thought of as the god of beginnings. Some think that one of the faces of Janus looks to the future, and the other is looking at the past. As we celebrate New Year's, many of us look back at the year that was, and make promises to ourselves about the year to come.

February is named after Februa, the Roman feast of purification held on the fifteenth of the second month. It's also the time when everybody seems to head for the south to escape the winter chills. March refers to the war god Mars, probably due to the stormy nature of the month.

Most of the months we take for granted have some kind of Roman reference as their origin: June from the goddess Juno, July from Julius Caesar, August from the Emperor Augustus, September from the Latin number for seven, and so forth. The Roman Empire has been dead for a number of years, but we are stilled ruled by their calendar.

The Jewish calendar begins with a 30-day period of time called Tishri. Rosh Hashanah and Yom Kippur fall during this month, which the Roman calendar calls September. This is regarded as the birth month of Abraham, Isaac, and Jacob, and its zodiacal sign is a set of scales, symbolizing the weighing of one's deeds between the New Year and the Day of Atonement.

Hanukkah begins on the twenty-fifth day of Kislev, a time symbolized by the zodiacal sign of the archer, the emblem of Benjamin. The festive season of Hanukkah is followed by Tebet, which has a fast on the tenth day. The zodiacal sign of Tebet is the goat, the emblem of Dan. It seems that no matter what the calendar, a time of feasting is followed by a fast, a moral belt tightening.

Shebat represents a new year for trees, a kind of arbor day, on the fifteenth. It was believed that demons roamed the earth during this month, and the zodiacal sign is the water bearer, the emblem of Asher.

As any one who does crossword puzzles knows, the next month is Adar, a period of time which commemorates the birth and death of Moses, the feast of Esther, and on the fourteenth day, Purim. This month is followed by Nisan, the month of Passover, which begins on the fifteenth day. The entire month is regarded as a prolonged festival and blessed month in which to die, even though no public mourning is permitted. Its zodiac sign is the ram, the emblem of Judah. These months are followed by Lyar, Sivan,Tammuz, Ab, and Elul, all of which have some reference to the Old Testament or the history of the Jewish people, as well as a zodiacal emblem.

For those of the Islamic faith, Ramadan, the holiest period of the year, will soon be upon us. One of the five pillars of the Islamic faith, Ramadan is a month of fasting. From dawn until dusk throughout the month, the faithful go without food, drink, or sexual intercourse. It is the ninth month of the Islamic year, the time when "the Koran was sent down as a guidance for the people," and is seen more as an obedient reponse to a command from God than as a time of atonement. It is also the time when many of the faithful make their way on a pilgrimage to Mecca, the birthplace of Muhammad.

The first month of the Islamic year is Muharram. The first day of this calendar was July 16, 622, in the Western or Roman calendar. This month is followed by Safar and Rabi I, which celebrates Muhammad's birthday on the twelfth; Rabi II, which notes the birthday of el Hoseyn, Muhammad's son, on the twelfth day; Jumada I and Jumada II; Rajab, when on the twelfth day, Muhammad's ascension to Heaven is celebrated;

Sha'ban; and Ramadan, the holiest period of the Islamic year. Ramadan is followed by Shawwal, Dhu'l-Qa, and Dhu'l-Hijja, during which Kurban, commemorating Abraham's attempt to sacrifice Isaac, is celebrated for three or four days.

All of these calendars have one thing in common: they believe in a kind of absolute time. Each event in history could be labeled by a number, and depending on your faith, you could agree on the time interval between events, even accounting for "leap years."

When Einstein came on the scene, time became a personal thing, relative to the individual who measured it. It has turned out that the laws of science do not distinguish between the past and the future. Thinkers like Einstein, Richard Feynman, and Stephen Hawking talk about entropy, where disorder increases with time. Hawking talks about the arrow of time, something that distinguishes the past from the future, giving a direction to time. He says there are at least three different arrows of time: the thermodynamic, or the direction of time in which disorder increases; the psychological, the direction in which we feel time passes, the direction in which we remember the past but not the future; and finally, the cosmological, the direction of time in which the universe is expanding rather than contracting. Maybe we need a calendar to show these phenomena.

As we approach the millenium, we seem to be entering a new age of belief; it was reported recently that more people have faith in something. So as we put away our Christmas past and present, and look to the future, the passage of time does not seem so threatening after all.

Posing for a Portrait

I've never thought of myself as model material. The older I get, the less time I want to spend in front of a mirror. The secret of having a beard is that it not only hides one's mug, but weeks may pass before one has to confront those sagging jowls and saddle bag eyes and do a little trimming of the facial hair.

So when a friend from the South Bay Art Association portrait group asked me to pose, my first response was loud and visceral: "You've gotta be kidding!"

She went on to explain that the group meets on odd Tuesdays, and is constantly on the lookout for "new and interesting faces."

Actually, the request came at a good time. The newspaper was in that black hole between elections and Thanksgiving, an op-ed vacuum as it were, so I was looking for material. Also, Christmas was looming in the near distance, and a portrait might make a good present for a sister in New Mexico or a wife in Brookhaven. I couldn't think of anyone else who would appreciate such a gift. With some reservations, I agreed to the sitting.

For someone who is unable to stay at one place for more than five minutes, sitting for over two hours would be a challenge. To be sure, the arrangement called for a five-minute break after each fifteen minutes, but I wasn't sure I would be able to sit absolutely still for fifteen minutes at a stretch.

Sitting there on an improvised throne, staring at a spot on the wall as instructed, I suddenly realized that twenty pairs of eyes were staring at me. I suddenly felt incredibly self-conscious, convinced that they were staring at the tiny zit that had appeared on the end of my nose that morning.

One or two had their hand in the air, holding a pencil or a brush, and I resisted the urge to call on them.

Suddenly, I realized that they were not looking at me as a person, but as an object, a mass of atoms and molecules taking up space. I could have been a squash, for all they cared. However, they weren't doing still lifes today.

The first fifteen minutes seemed like an eternity. I was beginning to think I would never be able to move again when the kitchen timer sounded and everyone broke for Oreos and coffee.

The five-minute break seemed to be over in seconds, and we were at it again after a brief debate: some of the artists wanted my glasses off. The glasses-on contingent carried the day, to my relief. To have to sit still and not be able to see would be too much to bear.

A little more at ease, I retreated to the inner space of my mind. The music from National Public Radio, mostly classical, helped as I withdrew into a Zen-like trance. At one point, I could hear the voice of my Yankee mother-in-law, repeating one of her New England sayings: "You can get used to hanging, if you hang long enough."

Each fifteen-minute session seemed to get shorter and shorter. The music switched from a string quartet to a piano concerto. During the breaks after the first hour, I started to take a look at the various renderings. I was pleasantly surprised. These folks, mostly retired, were no amateurs. Mentally, I selected one or two potential Christmas presents. As we chatted, I noticed that many of them were looking at me intently. It's not that our conversation was that scintillating, they were just getting a closer look at the subject, from a different perspective.

As we reached the end of the second hour, a line from T.S. Eliot crossed my mind, "In the room the women come and go, talking of Michelangelo." Then I remembered where that refrain came from: "The Love Song of J. Alfred Prufrock," a rather sad verse about a middle-aged man looking in front of a mirror, wondering what had happened to his youth.

About Libraries

In western New York, there is a place where people go for intellectual refreshment and cultural renewal, a place where you can take a course, sit under a tree and read a book, and attend a concert at night. It is called Chautauqua.

As I look over the latest edition of the South Country Library Notes, with its announcements of upcoming concerts, income tax assistance, storytelling, crafts programs, book discussions, and so forth, I am struck by the comparison. For all of us, whether we live in Moriches or Bellport or Patchogue, the public library is our Chautauqua.

And more.

For the child without a computer, our version of Chautauqua is a way to get on the internet. For the senior citizen living on limited means, it is a way to read the latest best-seller without having to buy it. For the writer and the student, it is a source for research. For the artist, it is a place to exhibit his or her paintings. For the music lover, it is an ongoing source of pleasure.

The library also provides talking books to William, a veteran in East Patchogue who is blind, and to Sarah, a resident of North Bellport who is paralyzed from the neck down, as well as to many other people who qualify for them.

In Patchogue, the library will even provide you with a fishing pole. You have to supply your own bait, however.

We also notice that there will be a South Country Library budget vote on March 22. While it is true that all those books, videos, tapes, programs, and services are free, the paradox is that somebody has to pay for them, and that somebody is the taxpayer.

47

We took a look at last year's tax statement, and saw that our library tax was about $250. Not bad, considering that we took out at least twice that amount in books, tapes, and CD's. That comes to about 68 cents a day, not a bad bargain in anyone's scheme of things.

The new tax rate is about two percent more, or for us, about $5, the cost of a half a tank of gas, which we will spend in the next three or four months driving to the library. That brings the daily cost up to 70 cents a day, still a pretty good deal.

We looked up an old brochure from Chautauqua, one that we examined when we were thinking about traveling to western New York a few years ago. The price tag for one week came to about $2,000, which included meals and lodging at the famed Atheneum, courses, and concerts.

The local library is looking better and better these days, all things considered.

About Sarah, Once More, with Feeling

As I head south for my winter vacation, my thoughts will turn to Sarah, who still lies on her back in a bed in North Bellport, just as she has remained for the last four years.

I promised her that I was not deserting her, just going on a vacation for awhile, and that I would be back to check up on her situation in January. Sarah's mother, who spends most of her days caring for her quadraplegic daughter, said, "I wish I could have a vacation."

My conscience is somewhat mollified by the improvements in Sarah's life in the last few weeks. The furnace has been fixed, so her family will have heat when the cold comes creeping through the damaged front door of the house. The roaches appear to have been exterminated, though one visitor from Social Services said he saw one crawling up the wall the other day, just over Sarah's head.

Speaking of Social Services, they and the Town of Brookhaven inspected the house last week, and the Town "found serious fire safety violations," condemning it as being unsafe for human habitation. I pondered over the wording of the letter that Sarah and her family had received: "...you are living in substandard housing that could present a serious danger to your health and safety. We are urging you to relocate immediately. If you need help in obtaining new housing, please go to the Social Services Center between the hours of..." I wondered how Sarah was going to accomplish that chore.

Since the conditions that prevail in the house did not spring up overnight, I also wondered where the inspectors had been before we started writing about Sarah.

I learned that Social Services had stopped the rent payments to the landlord, citing the conditions in the house as "dangerous, hazardous, and detrimental to life and health."

Social Services took Sarah's mother to inspect another house on nearby Michigan Avenue. It was a presentable little place, but there were several problems: there was no handicap ramp, no bathtub in which to bathe Sarah, and the doors were too narrow for Sarah's special wheelchair.

So the family continues to look for better housing. A number of people seem to be working on this problem: Charlie Stephani and the Kiwanis, Dennis Novak of Social Services, Ed Hernandez of Community Housing Innovations.

There is no handicap ramp at Sarah's present abode either, even though everyone from the Town of Brookhaven to county legislators have promised that one would be built.

Thanks to Kiwanis of Patchogue, the family has a new refrigerator-freezer, cablevision, and a sorely-needed telephone.

Thanks to the Hagerman Ambulance Company, Sarah was transported to the local elementary school, where she was able to see her son Shajee in a Christmas pageant.

Thanks to the Kiwanis, there are beds for everyone in the family, and Shajee will not have to sleep on a couch at the foot of his mother's bed.

Thanks to the South Country Lions and the Kiwanis wives, there are linens for the new beds.

Thanks to whoever it was who donated a 26-inch bike, and 50 gallons of fuel oil.

Thanks to the Suffolk County Library System and all the other folks who donated clothes, toys, and food baskets, making Christmas and Hanukah a little better for Sarah and her family. The food baskets are particularly welcome, for the family is no longer entitled to food stamps. It seems that the $330 a week job held by Elishaba, Sarah's sister, puts the family just over the limit that would entitle them to this benefit. Elishaba has two choices: stop working or move out on her own.

Sometimes it seems that the system encourages people to live on welfare.

And finally, thanks to Susan Weeks, Sarah's constant and faithful friend, who first called our attention to Sarah's plight, and who continues to fight fiercely on her behalf.

Meanwhile, the town, county, and state legislators continue to fret over Sarah's situation. Maybe by the time I get back from Florida, they will have done something about it.

Sarah: One Year Later

It has been almost a year since we first wrote about Sarah, the young mother who was paralyzed six years ago from the neck down in a drive-by shooting at a block party in North Bellport.

There's a saying, "The more things change, the more they remain the same," which seems to apply to Sarah's life in the last year.

Since last Thanksgiving, her life has improved somewhat, due to the efforts of the Patchogue Kiwanis, the Suffolk Library System, countless individuals who have donated money, clothing, food baskets, and on occasion, Social Services.

Typically, various local politicians have made promises to improve Sarah's situation, but have not followed up as much as one would hope they would. However, she still spends her days flat on her back, staring at four walls, listening to books on tape provided by the library system.

Sarah and her family have been moved to a house in Coram, secured by Social Services, which is rat and roach-free, and heated. Every member of the family—Sarah, her mother Fanny Moore, her son Shajee, and her sister Elishaba, who is expecting a child of her own in January—has a room of their own. No longer does Sarah have to face everyone who comes in the front door. If she wants, she can now spend an entire afternoon in her room with the door closed, lying under a cool sheet.

There is a big yard, with a lawn, where Shajee can romp with the family dog.

As much as Sarah's life has improved, there are still some problems.

A few weeks ago, medical transport workers were taking Sarah to rehabilitation when they dropped her on the Hoyle apparatus as they tried to move her from her room to the ambulance. Sarah hit her head and suffered what has been diagnosed as a concussion. Now, in a kind of Catch-22 situation, the medical transport service is unwilling to pick Sarah up to take her to the rehabilitation she needs so she can have an operation to "unfreeze" her arm, necessary to begin operating her wheelchair.

Just last week, after living in the house for several months, the family finally got a telephone. No longer does Sarah's mother have to run to the neighbors when there is an emergency.

Glenn Charrat, the new president of the Patchogue Kiwanis, is mustering a crew to build a wheelchair ramp at the new house, and is looking into a way to reconfigure the hallway so Sarah can be moved from her bed to an ambulance on a gurney.

Sarah reports that Shajee is doing well in his new school. In fact, papers and projects with grades from 70 to 90 are proudly displayed on the walls of her room.

In the basement, the washer and dryer donated by James Johnson of Toronto, Canada, hum as Fannie Moore washes Shajee's new school clothes.

Like any one else this time of year, Sarah and her family are looking forward to Thanksgiving and Christmas. They may not have a lot of money, but they have each other, and a new, warm home. As Sarah says, "We have a lot to be thankful for."

Valentine's Day: A Chance to be Young Again

Someone once said that the main attraction for Valentine's Day is that it gives us the opportunity to be young and foolish again. We're inclined to agree. The occasion allows us to say and do things we would not dream of doing the rest of the year. For example, it is one of the few times of the year that a man may go into a card, flower, or lingerie shop without looking over his shoulder.

In the spirit of the occasion, we have compiled a list of things to do on Valentine's Day that go beyond the traditional card and flowers and dinner at a fancy restaurant. Most of these activities don't cost very much, don't take much in the way of preparation, and are almost guaranteed to make our readers feel young and just a little bit foolish, which is what Valentine's Day is all about.

1. Go to an old-fashioned drug store, like the one on Main Street in Riverhead, and share an ice cream soda. There are several restaurants on Main Street in Patchogue that have counters and serve up a passable ice cream soda or egg cream if you don't want to go to Riverhead.

2. Go to the movies in the afternoon, and if the theater doesn't have a balcony, sit in the last row with a box of Jujubes and hold hands, and maybe even neck a little.

3. Go to Smith Point, take off your shoes and socks, roll up your pants, and run through the surf, holding hands. (We know it's cold, but that's part of the excitement.)

4. Get out some paste, glue, colored paper, and paper doilies, (all of which can be purchased at your local variety store), and make a Valentine for your partner, just as you did in elementary school.

5. Take a slow train to Montauk, just as you might have done on prom night, or if you feel like spending a little money, engage a limousine and tell the driver to take you to Montauk Point, in time for a sunrise.

6. Write a love note on lined school paper and fold it up so it can be passed across the classroom. Don't hesitate to use wild and fanciful hyperbole in the style of W.H. Auden: "I'll love you until the stars are hung out to dry, etc."

7. Take turns reading Shakespearean sonnets. There are 154 of them, so it might take you awhile. Or read Elizabeth Barrett Browning's "Sonnets from the Portuguese;" there aren't as many of them, but they are just as appropriate for the occasion.

8. Have a pillow fight, then kiss and make up. Or rent a bicycle for two and go for a ride in Hecksher Park.

9. Rent a romantic Disney video, like "Beauty and the Beast" or "The Little Mermaid." Make some popcorn for the occasion.

10. Go to a children's park and push your partner in a swing. This activity is guaranteed to bring a blush to the cheek of anyone over 30.

Well, there's our list. It isn't very long, but we left it that way on purpose, for we are sure that you have some ideas of your own.

Being on the Street Builds Character

We ran into the Hubcap King the other day. He was standing in front of the supermarket, smoking a cigar, looking like a retiree sneaking a smoke while his wife did the shopping.

I refer to him as the Hubcap King because he made a marginal living selling hubcaps at the side of the road. He usually had a display of about 20 odd hubcaps that had fallen by the wayside.

Things have not been going so well for Gilbert the Hubcap King, it turns out.

When I last reported on his activities, Gilbert was in the process of being removed from his squatter's roadside emporium by the police and the highway department. It seems the owner of the property did not look kindly on someone who appeared to be living in the woods behind his establishment.

"I've been on the street for the last couple of weeks," Gilbert said.

I asked him if he had called the number of the civil liberties lawyer I had given him a couple of weeks ago.

"I tried a couple of times," he said, "but all I got was a machine. She left a card at my old address."

The card and most of Gilbert's belongings are locked up at his old address, a rooming house, held in lieu of back rent.

Think about how hard it must be to make a telephone call when you're calling from the street, when you have to find five soda cans to redeem so you can get a quarter to call your lawyer. That is, of course, if you can find a pay phone that works.

I asked Gilbert what he did when the weather turned bad. "There's a lot of places," he said, declining to specify any exact locations. "There's places near the shopping malls, and along the railroad tracks. We keep dry."

"When you're on the street, you have a lot of time to kill, so you spend an hour or so at one bus stop, then, if you have the fare, take a ride, then sit at another bus stop for awhile Then you take a walk along the roadside, looking for bottles and cans. You can make $5-$10 a day on returns," Gilbert said.

The king has a couple of court dates coming up, to answer to charges of trespassing. "I've been spending a lot of time getting my head together," he said. "Besides, being on the street builds character."

Promises of Spring

There's something about that week between Groundhog Day and Valentine's Day, a promise of spring that quickens our blood. It may be that first breath of warm air blowing in from the south, bringing with it thoughts of gardening or walking on the beach. It may be the sight of senior citizens, poking their heads out of doors, taking those first tentative steps of a walk down the street one more time, one more year. It may be the slips of crocus shoots, poking through the snow on the south side of the house.

Other signs of an incipient spring, that it is not really winter as the calendar would have us believe: We clean off our golf clubs, thinking, "Maybe, just maybe, this will be the year that I break 100."

We order a new pair of khaki slacks from L.L. Bean, only to realize with some dismay that they have to be two sizes larger. We make promises to ourselves, reinforced by the diet advertising that seems to proliferate television programming these days, that this will be the year that we will not only break 100, but will also lose the twenty pounds that seem to have magically appeared on our bodies like some invaders from an alien planet. There is also a sudden yearning to buy a new car, preferably a convertible, and drive along the Ocean Parkway with the top down and the pony tail streaming in the breeze, a defiant banner against old age. We rummage throught the garage, looking for an old baseball glove, ostensibly to give to a grandchild, but secretly wishing to once again become one of the boys of spring, to feel the sunshine on our faces as we wander among the daisies in right field, waiting to chase down a descending orb.

As William Cullen Bryant said, "While slant sun of February pours into the bowers a flood of light."

Of course, all this talk of an early spring makes us look over our shoulder at the clouds gathering in the northwest, wondering if we have provoked the weather gods to bring us a February full of snow and ice. We are reminded of the Blizzard of '88 that took place in March.

Pennsylvania has its Pauxatawny Phil, Malvern its Mel (who is really from the Long Island Game Farm in Manorville, and should be called Manorville Mel). Even Brookhaven Lab is said to have Physics Phil, a marmot who, it is said, glows in the dark. We have all sorts of auguries and ways of predicting the weather, most of them unreliable.

Eric Sevareid, TV commentator, said, "Every American believes he possesses an equal and God-given expertise in three things: politics, religion, and the weather."

In Brookhaven, we have my neighbors Bob and Gloria Brown, retired meteorologists who have a weather station in their back yard. The Browns have been keeping track of the local weather for the last 25 years, and Bob says, "January of 1998 has been above normal in all categories of temperatures. The average maximum temperature for 1972-1997 is 38.3, and the average maximum for 1998 was 44.0; the average temperature for 1972-97 was 29.1, and for 1998, was 36.9. The total average precipitation in inches (rain) was 4.03 in 1972-97, and 6.05 in 1998. The total average snowfall in inches in 1972-97 is 7.00, and in 1998, 1.00. This means that January of 1998 had more rainfall than normal, and less snowfall."

We asked Bob how all of this had come about. He said, "There were several east coast storms whose contours passed south and east of Long Island. The tracks of these storms kept Long Island warm, wet, and free of most of the snow." He reminded us that February is the coldest month of the year in this area, but if the trend that may be caused by El Nino continues, we might get off lightly.

Let's hope he is right.

The Writing Life: A Tax Audit

I had an income tax audit recently. At that time, I tried to explain to the IRS that a writer's life often becomes material for his work, grist for the mill, fodder for the weekly demands of newspaper space.

Therefore, I argued, any expenses incurred on trips to Florida, Vermont, and the Appalachian Trail in 1996 should be deductible. The representative, a Ms. Helen Pattinson, didn't agree with me at first, but when I told her I was going to write a piece about my encounter with her and the IRS, she seemed to become more sympathetic to my plight. By the end of the audit, she wanted me to send her a copy of the article, and spelled her name out for me.

I knew I was in trouble when my tax man, who was supposed to have accompanied me, called from the hospital the day before the audit. "I'm afraid you're on your own," he told me.

I arrived at the IRS offices in Riverhead about an hour early, and sat in the parking lot brooding about my ailing accountant and his inability to support me in my hour of need.

When the doors opened, I was shown to Ms. Pattinson's office. I expected to be greeted by the Wicked Witch from the Wizard of Oz, with fiendish grin, rubbing her hands in anticipation of picking me clean. What I got was not quite the fairy godmother, but she was smiling and not unsympathetic to my cause. It turned out that she was married to a history teacher in a local high school, who was about to retire with her to Hawaii, so I felt we had some rapport.

As we worked our way through the twisted state of my 1996 return, she gave me some advice and commented on the audit process. "It's a good thing you kept a diary and a travel journal," she said, "some people show up with their hands in their pockets, with no documentation, and try to argue their way out of the situation. At least you have some records and cancelled checks."

I had the receipts from our Florida trip, when I had started filing "postcard" articles by e-mail to the newspaper. I didn't have any documentation for the trips to Vermont and the Appalachian Trail, but I had the articles. Amazingly, she allowed my expenses on those trips.

At the beginning of the interview, Ms. Pattinson had taken a narrative account of who I was and what I did. She even asked questions about my wife and our children. That narrative turned out to be significant, because she matched that to the events in my date book and the financial side of my life. "Everything matched up," she said, "which proved your credibility. For example, you said you and your wife delivered for Meals on Wheels every Thursday, and that notation was in your datebook."

Another piece of advice: if you are a writer, keep all your writing accounts separately. Deposit all income from writing in a separate bank account, and get a special credit card to use for writing expenses.

As we approached the end of the second hour of the interview, I began to realize I was getting a lesson in tax finances. I was heartened when the auditor said, "Your case is not so bad. I had someone who owned us over $100,000. He wasn't able to pay, so we settled for about ten percent of the original amount."

I also realized I was seeing the new face of the Internal Revenue Service, an agency that is trying to promote a user-friendly image.

At the end of our session, Ms. Pattinson reminded me to keep complete and separate records from now on.

She also reminded me, in a friendly way, that I still owed the IRS some money for 1996.

Hateful Things

What happens to us when we turn 65? That particular transition in life seems to be more portentous than those that precede or follow, and it doesn't have to do with Social Security or Medicare.

A lot of people who turn 65 find themselves compiling lists of hateful things, and really don't care what other people think of them for doing so. Maybe it comes with the territory.

We find ourselves wishing dire calamities on individuals who commit hateful acts. For example, we wish a severe case of laryngitis on the person who feels compelled to talk for the duration of a movie, or for the dentist who, after packing our mouths with cotton wadding, asks, "Seen any good movies lately?'

May the driver who always runs a red light on Nicoll's Road, as well as the driver who tailgates us on the Sunrise Highway at 7:00 a.m., be visited by a monthful of flat tires on the Long Island Expressway--at rush hour.

Woe unto the person who enters the supermarket express line with more than ten items and a checkbook in hand!

To the person who enters a crowded elevator and proceeds to sneeze without covering his face, we wish a perpetually stuffed nose.

May a debilitating computer virus strike the folks who keep loading up our e-mail with offers to get rich quick or enjoy a fabulous sex life.

A case of fleas has been reserved for those dog owners who allow their pets to run loose.

We wish a permanent condition of writer's cramp for those folks who send unsigned letters to the editor.

Like Dante's Inferno, we have reserved punishments for particular sins against humanity: a special place in hell should be set aside for those people who dump illegally in wild life refuges, or anywhere else, for that matter.

There's an address in the netherworld for graffiti writers, sort of like the punishment in Kafka's "Penal Colony," where the writer's "tag" is etched into his body, slowly and painfully.

There's also room for the drivers of the latest behemoth who shoulders us out of the way on the roads, as well as the waiter who persists in serving us with his thumb in our soup.

As for the person who smiles like an idiot and tells us to have a nice day--watch out!

So what do we do to get out of this 65-year-old funk? After all, we don't want to spend the rest of our lives grousing about everything. Weren't there a couple of movies recently about grouchy old men?

Here's a list of things that have helped us to look on the bright side of things, offered in the spirit of public service. When you're going somewhere, take the back roads, the scenic route. Go to a silly movie, and laugh a little. When the circus comes to town, take a child to see it. Look up at the sky once a day, sunset or sunrise. Take a walk on the beach, and look for beach glass. Read the comic strips. Go shopping, buy a colorful tie or scarf. Go bowling in the afternoon.

Last but not least, make a list of grateful things.

A St. Patrick's Day Meditation

Around this time of year, everyone likes to think they are Irish, even folks with names that end in vowels wind up wearing green shirts or ties, and participating in the annual St. Patrick's Day rituals. Attendance at local colleges and places of business drops drastically, as students and workers swell the crowds in New York, Huntington, Rocky Point, and other celebrations.

I like to think that I have a touch of the old sod in my bones: there's what used to be red hair on my head, a quick temper, an affinity for ale, and a love of words.

My favorite writer is James Joyce, my favorite poet is William Butler Yeats, and the Irish playwright Sean O'Casey speaks to my soul.

I have watched "The Quiet Man" many times over, as well as "Finian's Rainbow," and whenever an advertisement for *Riverdance* appears on the television, my toes begin to twitch. Moreover, my favorite color is green.

Most of my boyhood friends were Irish-American. First, there were the brothers George and John. George and I played high school football together. He could throw a football pass that looked like a rope stretched between his hand and the receiver. Since I was always a bit nearsighted and he had no patience for fumblers, many a time he would bounce a pass off my helmet, just to show his displeasure. John, the non-athlete, was the team manager. Their father owned the Hotel Nyack, and on St. Patrick's Day, we always wound up in the bar, drinking green beer provided by himself. In the years that passed, John became a postal clerk, and George became an alcoholic, stuck in the time warp of his former gridiron glory.

Then there were the Henry twins, Patrick and Norman. No kidding, Patrick Henry. They didn't drink in high school because they wanted to stay in shape for wrestling. However, every St. Patrick's Day was special for them and their friends, because it meant a big, sit-down dinner to soda bread, corned beef, and cabbage, Irish soul food.

These friends helped me to connect with an uncertain heritage, lost in an orphanage many years ago. As they defined their background, their roots, they let me in, let me share their Irishness, and for that I am grateful to them, wherever they are.

Erin go bragh!

To Be a Volunteer

Last week a couple of Meals-on-Wheels volunteers discovered one of their clients, a woman in her nineties who lived with her little dog, lying on the floor of her apartment in Bellport, unable to move. It seems that the woman had fallen out of bed and broken her hip.

The rescue wasn't easy. First the volunteers had to find the owner of the apartment to get the key. Then they had to unscrew the chain bolt to get into the apartment. Meanwhile, one of them called 911, which brought the local ambulance company, manned by volunteers, into the operation. Finally, something had to be done about the dog, which was placed with a caring neighbor.

This is not the first time this has happened to Meals-on-Wheels volunteers, who not only deliver warm, healthy meals to the old and the infirm, but also spend a little time with them, chatting about the weather and other inconsequential matters, and in cases like this, serve as a lifeline in case medical help is needed. Unfortunately, there are more potential clients than there are drivers.

Meals-on-Wheels is not the only organization that needs volunteers, someone who is willing to donate one or two hours a week helping others.

In a time of shrinking social services, the need for people who are willing to give a little time and energy in the service of humanity is greater than ever before.

Maybe part of the problem is that many potential volunteers come from the "me" generation, baby boomers who are too busy chasing the sun or a golf ball or the elusive dream of a perfect body to bother with other people. What they don't realize is that there is somebody out there who is lonely, who would enjoy a brief visit and a warm meal.

There is somebody out there who wants to learn how to read, waiting for a Literacy Volunteer to open a world of ideas and travel to the foreign places of the mind.

There is someone out there who lives too far from a bus stop, who needs a Red Cross driver to give him a lift and a little fellowship.

There is a patient lying in the hospital, waiting for a volunteer to bring her a magazine or some flowers, someone to break the monotony of the hospital routine.

There are the blind, waiting for a new guide dog to be raised and trained, or waiting for someone to read the latest best-seller onto tape.

There is a child, struggling with his homework, who needs someone to look over his shoulder and point the way to academic success. The new Regents mandate is not just going to require a massive re-tooling of the educational process at no small expense; it will require a cadre of volunteers who will help the youngsters to read, write, and compute.

There are soup kitchens, food pantrys, wildlife habitats, neighborhood cleanup groups: the list goes on and on.

We are reminded of the Bellport High School student who showed up at the Habitat for Humanity housebuilding project on Carver Boulevard last year, hammer in hand and hope in her heart. At the end of the day, she was still pounding nails with two hands, as the hammer got heavier and her blisters got larger. She was sunburned and tired, but there was an exultant gleam in her eyes, and we knew she would be back the next day to finish the job.

She could have spent the weekend flipping hamburgers so she could raise enough money for the latest lip gloss, but somehow, we feel that helping out with the Habitat project, working side by side with the new owner, was a bit more satisfying.

Of course, she was back the next day. That's what it means to be a volunteer.

On Gardening

There's something about spring that brings out the gardener in me. As the daffodils and croci begin to emerge from their blanket of leaves, I find myself looking at seed catalogues, and pausing on the road to see if the garden center has opened yet. My little four by eight planting box in the backyard trembles with anticipation, or is it fear?

The problem is that I am not, nor have I ever been, a gardner. I suppose it comes from spending the first two years of my life in Brooklyn, where the only gardens are in window boxes, and in New Jersey, ironically called "the Garden State," (Have you driven through Bayonne lately?), where at a tender age I was coerced into weeding and tilling something called a

"Victory Garden." The few puny carrots and bedraggled lettuce that made a reluctant appearance did little to contribute to the war effort.

I managed to stay away from the good earth for a number of years, until we moved to our own place on Long Island. My next door neighbor talked me into helping him to clear about a half-acre of woods behind our houses, involving a couple of backbreaking months of tree cutting and brush clearing. I was really excited about the pioneering spirit of the whole thing. Cultivate your own garden, Candide! My blisters felt honorable and manly. On his side of the patch, my neighbor planted strawberries, potatoes, and tomatoes. I planted corn and peanuts, much to the pleasure of the local wildlife population. Occasionally, I would sneak over to my neighbor's side of the garden and sample a strawberry or two. He is a generous-hearted fellow, and didn't seem to mind.

I think our joint effort at gardening began to decline when, in a never-ending race to keep up with each other, we installed swimming pools in our respective back yards. The time we used to spend weeding and watering was now devoted to skimming, cleaning, and balancing the Ph level, what ever that is. On top of that, my spouse and I re-discovered golf, an activity that keeps me out of the garden for hours at a time.

However, once a new resident built a house across the street and started a garden, my neighbor deserted me and our weedy patch for greener pastures. Once in awhile, while walking the dog, I would look over their fence longingly.

Everything was properly staked, mulched, watered regularly. The cabbages and heads of lettuce stood at attention, the tomatoes were full and ripe on their vines, and there were no weeds raising their ugly heads. It was a garden that would make Martha Stewart proud.

Not to be outdone, I installed my little four by eight kitchen garden, built up from the ground by interlocking 4X4's and filled with good, rich soil, compost, and mulch.

Every spring, I would plant my peas, radishes, carrots, tomatoes, and other salad vegetables, reveling in the fecund, moist earth between my fingers. For the first month, I would water and weed religiously. Then, just as it began to get warm, we would head off to Italy or France or some other foreign destination. By the time we returned, the garden would have died a lonely death, untended, unheralded, and unmourned.

Last year, I tried a technique learned at the Hamlet Organic Garden, where they have no trouble growing all kinds of delectable things. I followed the old Indian method of planting a fish head, a bean, a squash seed, and a corn kernel. For some reason, we had a lot of feline visitors in the next couple of nights, but I don't think they found the fish heads. I think the idea is that the bean, the squash, and the corn are supposed to help each other out, all gaining nutrients from the fish head. Well, the squash vines came out, flowered briefly, and quickly dried out. The corn stalks shot up, but only produced one ear of corn, hardly enough for half a cup of popcorn. We never saw any beans. I guess it worked for the Indians, but it's a good thing we don't have to depend on my garden for sustenance.

The only thing I have ever planted successfully is bamboo. About thirty-five years ago, I saw some bamboo growing over at Bartlett Lake in Middle Island. After making some inquiries, I found out that a Captain Bartlett, a seafaring amateur botanist, brought back many exotic plants from his travels and tried them out on Long Island. Evidently, he brought a species of bamboo back from the Orient one time, and it took to the sandy soil and moderate climate of the island, which is on the same latitude as Japan. I dug up a single root, about six inches long, and planted it out next to the garage, and promptly forgot about it. Nothing happened the first year. Then, after a particularly rainy spring, these giant stalks began appearing in the side yard. In a few short years, we had a bamboo jungle running along the western side of our property, and it continues to grow every spring, no matter how much we (and our next door neighbors) hack away at it. It has become a source for snapper fishermen, other gardeners, and the itinerant flute maker. The other day, my other neighbor, my former gardening partner, asked me if he could grind up some of the bamboo to use as mulch for his pristine garden.

I hope he gets bugs.

Buying a Car

Every three or four years, we get the irresistible urge to buy a new car. It must be the massive advertising campaigns that promise us a more exciting life if we purchase the latest model of a vehicle characterized by a superfluity of superlatives: faster, wider, bigger, better, sexier. On top of all their virtues, these new cars always seem to be going through water or climbing mountains.

We promised ourselves that this year it would be different. We would resist the siren songs of the advertising world, and stick with our reliable, trusty Honda Civic sedan. We would refuse to buy something that costs twice as much as we paid for our house thirty-five years ago. We got the oil changed in the Honda, bought a couple of new tires, and were prepared to add another 15,000 miles to the odometer.

Then one day, a week or so ago, we must have suffered some kind of minor stroke and forgotten all of our resolve. We found ourselves in an auto showroom, looking at something called an Outback Sport.

It may have been some kind of reaction to a recent visit to the hospital, for there was something life-affirming about considering the possibilities of a four-wheel drive vehicle, complete with spoiler and electric windows, that took corners like a race car and bespoke an aura of youthfulness. Maybe that's another reason we feel compelled to buy a new car every once in awhile: to hold off the advancing years for just a little bit.

Armed with the latest information from the internet and the hit radio show "Car Talk," we entered negotiations with an affable salesman, who assured us that the price he was giving us was unbeatable. We were also impressed by the fact that he did not call us by our first names, as most car salesmen are wont to do. We went to another dealer. The salesman there, after two disappearances to "talk to the manager," said he could offer us the same car for $600 less, if we ordered the car that day. Each time he returned, the heavy smell of cigarette smoke permeated his clothes, which led us to believe that "talking to the manager" meant having a smoke in the men's room. Feeling hustled, we returned to the first dealer.

He seemed glad to see us, and before going on a test drive, insisted that we look at the engine. Now, showing an automobile engine to your average English teacher is like explaining heart surgery to an Australian aborigine. To us, the working of an internal combustion engine, that we are being propelled at sixty miles an hour by a series of explosions, has always been kind of a mystery, like television pictures that fly through the air and travel along a piece of wire.

I kicked the tires, forgetting that that's what you're supposed to do with a used car. In fact, why do we kick the tires anyway?

After the test drive, the rationalizations began: we needed this car because it had much more cargo space, enough to carry a Welsh Terrier and an Airedale that seemed to be doubling in size every other week; we could afford it because I had just gotten a five percent raise; La Nina promises to bring us a winter of snow and ice, just the thing for four-wheel drive.

Then there was that new car smell. It's odd, no matter what kind of car we look at, unless it has leather upholstery, and we tend not to look at cars with leather, the new car smell permeates. It is as if the auto manufacturers are supplied with a aerosol can called "New Car Smell," and some person on the assembly line has the job of spraying the car, whatever it is, with new car smell.

Our youngest son, the artist, took one look at the spoiler on the front hood, and gave us the thumbs up sign. Our oldest son, the policeman, said we should have purchased something call "LoJack," because we had purchased the car that people would want to steal. I guess that was a compliment. Fellow workers said, "Congratulations." I don't know why people feel the need to congratulate us for going into hock for the next couple of years. Maybe they think we're doing so well, we could afford to buy a new car outright.

We wish that were the case.

In Celebration of Arbor Day

Tomorrow is Arbor Day, a day of celebration for tree-huggers everywhere. Actually, the idea of honoring our leafy friends goes back centuries, to ancient England, when the Druids cut the holy mistletoe from the revered oak trees with their golden sickles in preparation for sacrificing the village virgin.

When I think of Arbor Day, I remember those dumb ceremonies we used to have in elementary school in northern New Jersey.

In the middle of civics class, we would march out, single file, no talking, to the playground, to stand around a sapling the school custodian had just planted. The smartest kid in the class, usually a girl with pigtails and braces, would recite a poem by Joyce Kilmer, another famous New Jerseyan. I don't remember ever seeing anything else written by him. Maybe he was a one-poem man.

The trouble is that the tree was planted right in the middle of the playground, in what we knew as centerfield.

I don't know if the custodian, a gentleman from Czechoslovakia, where they don't know about baseball, was aware of his error, or if he just thought we could not hit the ball that far.

We spent the rest of the spring dodging the struggling tree, and occasionally crashing into it. One fellow in our class, who went on to play a couple of seasons with the New York Yankees, was so good at the bat that he could aim a hit in the direction of the tree, thus insuring extra bases as we ducked and weaved around the fledgling foliage. It was a wonder that the tree survived, but somehow it managed to endure.

A few years ago, I returned to my home town and paid a visit to the elementary school where I learned to appreciate words by copying all the entries for a letter in the dictionary. That was the principal's punishment of choice: if you were late, you copied all the l's, for example.

The principal was long gone, retired to dictionary heaven, or perhaps the other locale that begins with an H.

I walked out to the school yard, the scene of my first tastes of sweet triumph and bitter defeat, only to find that our playing field had been paved over with asphalt.

I looked out into centerfield, and there stood our tree from that ancient Arbor Day, standing tall and strong in a little patch of dirt.

Maybe that's what Long Island will look like some day, with little stands of green space in acres and acres of black tar.

In Praise of Secretaries

Yesterday was Professional Secretaries Day, which falls in the middle of Professional Secretaries Week, or to be politically correct, we should say Professional Administrative Assistants Week.

Whatever he or she is called, there is no office that is able to function effectively without these stalwarts.

Professional Secretaries Week is not a recent celebration, invented by the greeting card companies or a bunch of overworked and underpaid office assistants. It was founded over 40 years ago by Harry F. Klemfuss, a post-World War II publicist who worked for Young and Rubicam Advertising and who believed that the professional secretaries of America had struggled too long in the shadows of Rosie the Riveter.

Klemfuss's purpose, according to a *New York Times* article on June 3, 1952, was to encourage young women to enter the secretarial field and to demonstrate the importance of the "unhonored, unsung, and unrecognized" secretary of the day. He said, "I got sore because everybody paid tribute to Rosie the Riveter. Why not our secretaries, those wonderful gals."

Why not, indeed. There is a commercial running on TV these days where the secretary has gone to an office supply place and the boss is trying to run the copy machine in her absence. In the classic case of the employer as the bungling fool, he manages to cover himself with copy machine toner and run off 10,000 copies instead of 10. The secretary shows up, and he says to her, "There's something wrong with that machine," implying that it is now up to her to make things right.

We have a couple of such persons here at the newspaper. They know how to run all the machines: the copier, the fax machine, the telephone system, the computers. In addition to answering the telephone and greeting customers at the front desk (while preventing the local crazies from getting in to see us), they sell classified advertising and keep track of just about everything that goes on in the office. Without them, this place would fall apart in less than the time it takes to write this sentence. We are eternally grateful for their presence, even though the word "secretary" does not actually appear in their job description.

I think of other secretaries I have known and admired. There is Florence, without whom the acting superintendent of the local school District, would not be able to function as effectively as he does. There is the secretary of the local board of education, who must have the patience of a saint to sit through meeting after meeting, hour after hour, year after year. I can think of a lot more interesting ways to spend a Wednesday night, but Joan never complains, and she always seems to know what is going on.

Speaking of school systems, did you ever know of a school, elementary, middle, or high school, that could operate without the services of a front office secretary? Let's face it, most school administrators do not have an aptitude for bus schedules, telephone numbers, obscure rules and files, and they rely heavily on their secretarial staff to remember the names of the students in their charge.

In a way, the secretary is the closest thing to a mother in the business world. She keeps us properly dressed and reminds us when to eat; she keeps track of all the important birthdays and anniversaries; she knows where everything is; and she serves as conscience, advisor, confidant, and cheerleader.

So let us pay homage to secretaries everywhere. Where would we be without them? Still trying to figure out how the fax machine works, that's where.

A Few Thoughts on Fathers' Day

When I heard about my oldest son's idea for a Father's Day gift, I panicked. It turns out he had decided to take me out to lunch. When I heard the invitation, I thought, "What in the world are we going to talk about?"

It occurred to me that it had been a long time since I had a conversation of more than five minutes with any of my sons.

The last time my oldest son and I really talked was when he was in the Coast Guard. He couldn't get leave for the holidays, so I drove down to Baltimore and we celebrated Christmas in a motel near the base. He had gotten a two-hour break, and we exchanged presents and talked about his life in the service. I remember it because we had to say everything we wanted to say in two hours. The ride home seemed to take forever, as I replayed our conversation in my mind.

Since then, our talk has been around projects: building a deck, putting in a driveway, things like that, and the usual exchange of information about health and jobs. That's what fathers and sons do, mostly, exchange information, report to each other about sports, the weather, work, things like that. Guy talk.

It's pretty much the same with my other sons. We talk when we do things together: going to the movies, hitting golf balls, hiking, parallel activities where we can talk without looking each other in the eye. I must admit, however, that we have been talking more lately. Maybe that's a sign we are all growing up.

In *Our Town*, Thornton Wilder says that the relationship between a father and son is the "awkwardest" thing in the world. It really shouldn't be, for we have so much in common. Maybe that's part of the scheme of things. Having lived during the years that they are experiencing, starting out as a parent, beginning a career, finding their way, I know what they are going through, and they know that I know.

To complicate things further, we spend at least a third of our lives trying to please our fathers: learning how to fish when we loathe the cleaning, trying to throw a perfect curve ball when we would rather be reading a comic book, winning a wrestling match, becoming a department chairman.

Moreover, we all begin to realize at some point that our fathers are not as smart, strong, brave, clever as we once thought they were. Gone are the days when we used to wrestle in the living room, throw a football in the front yard, dunk each other in the swimming pool. They couldn't do those things now if their lives depended on it, and their growing fallibility saddens us.

Every Father's Day, the obligatory photograph is taken as my sons and I stand in the same place on the deck by the swimming pool. Looking at the pictures taken over the years, I notice that I seem to be shrinking, even though I am still six feet tall and weigh over 200 pounds. I wonder: will I continue to diminish in the next 25 years? Probably, but it feels strange to stand next to these giants that I once held in my hands and carried on my shoulders.

The photograph of my father that I carry around in my head was taken before I was born. He is standing on the slope of a Swiss alp during a post-college trip to Europe, his passage earned by playing the violin on a luxury liner, his tan a healthy contrast to the white shirt and white flannel pants and snow. He stands there, a young god with his movie star looks, ready to take on the future. That's how I like to remember him, before the years of work and family and responsibility and growing old.

Finally, there is the father's wish that we could have done more for our children. We often feel that we have let them down in one way or another, that we should have gone the extra distance in making them do their homework, insisting on the right school, career move, and so forth. We spend nights playing the insomniac's game of "woulda-shoulda-coulda."

Maybe the best thing we can do for them is set a good example, show them how to grow into old age gracefully. And, as someone once said, "The most important thing a father can do for his children is love their mother."

On Lawn Maintenance

Recently my spouse and I celebrated our mid-sixties by deciding to mow our own lawn.

After all, as Thornton Wilder says in *Our Town*, "one man in ten thinks it's a privilege to mow his own lawn." Besides, it would be a good source of cardio-vascular exercise, a matter of some interest for folks our age.

Dismissing the young man who, as it turned out, had plenty of work at the new golf course in Yaphank and was just doing us a favor, we started looking for a new lawn mower. First big decision: while it was axiomatic that we would be getting a gas-powered machine, would it be ride-on, self-propelled, or push?

The ride-on version seemed to defeat the purpose of our decision. Besides, it cost as much as a small car and would not fit in our already crowded garage.

A demonstration of the self-propelled mower was just as intimidating: I could see myself huffing and puffing as I raced to keep up with a machine that hurtled around the yard. Our intent was to prevent heart attacks, not cause them.

Finally we decided on an average-sized push mower, one that we could both start and handle with a modicum of stress.

Next decision: who was going to mow the lawn? In a era of gender equality, we decided to take turns.

Then came another question. What pattern would we follow? Back and forth in straight lines, or around the perimeter in an ever-shrinking circle? There's a fellow on our street, a retired police officer, who keeps an immaculate lawn that looks like the Yankee Stadium infield, mowed in a crisscross pattern.

Other considerations: should we seed and fertilize, or just let nature take its course? In its present condition, our lawn is a patchwork of seed types. For many years, I would re-seed the parts worn thin as a result of serving as home plate. Lately, since the boys have grown up and moved out, we left everything up to our former lawn service.

My spouse, a Virgo, frets about the condition of the lawn; I, an Aries, am inclined to leave things as they are. I think it's obscene that Americans spend more on their lawns than the gross national product of most Third World countries.

A book that was popular in the sixties, *Zen and the Art of Motorcycle Maintenance*, has just been re-published. It's more about traveling and finding yourself than fixing motorcycles, as I recall. As I walk around in circles on my front lawn, pushing my new lawn mower, I realize there is a Zen aspect of lawn maintenance. Mowing one's own lawn, mindlessly pushing a machine in slowly shrinking, concentric circles, creates an opportunity for contemplation. The steady hum of the machine drowns out the sounds of civilization. The sun is warm on my neck, and there is a certain satisfaction in following a line of cut grass.

I am glad we decided to mow our own lawn, but check with me again in the middle of the summer.

Memorial Day

During the Memorial Day services at the village cemetery in our home town, our thoughts traveled to another cemetery, at another time, another place.

There is a well-traveled road right off Route D514, which runs between Colleville-sur-Mer and St. Laurent-sur-Mer in Normandy. It leads to the American Military Cemtery and Memorial, located on a cliff right above Omaha Beach and the English Channel.

The cliff and beach were quiet at the time of our visit, but a look at the battle scenes of such movies as "The Longest Day" and "Saving Private Ryan" may give succeeding generations in idea of what it must have been like to survive that particular hell, or not to survive it.

The 172.5-acre cemetery contains the graves of 9,386 soldiers, including 307 who are unknown, each marked by a plain, white marble cross or Star of David. These simple headstones stand in crisp, white rows on neatly clipped lawns, as if at attention for one final time.

A closer look reveals two crosses where a father and son lie side by side. In thirty other instances, brothers lie next to brothers.

Near the entrance, there is a special plaque embedded in the cement, commemorating the journalists who covered the invasion.

Just down the road, there is another cemetery, with German names on the headstones. On D-Day, there are almost as many visitors there as there are to the American Cemetery.

When NBC newscaster Tom Brokaw walked the beaches of Normandy, he began to realize how the American men and women who grew up in the Great Depression, who came of age in World War II, shaped his life. The experience moved him to write a book called *The Greatest Generation*, a collection of letters written from the front lines during the war, or from families to their loved ones in harm's way in distant places. It's worth reading, along with such books as *Americans at War* by Stephen E. Ambrose and *Flags of Our Fathers* by James Bradley.

Some may consider it unfashionable to be patriotic, but we owe it to ourselves to visit such places and read such books, for it is important to remember the sacrifices that our fathers and uncles, mothers and aunts, and grandparents made so that we are able to celebrate the sometimes elusive concept we call "Freedom."

We owe something to the men and women who preserved it for us, too.

Notes from a Hospital Bed

Instead of hiking on the Appalachian Trail last week, I found myself walking the halls of Brookhaven Memorial Hospital, recovering from a sudden intestinal infection.

Beyond brooding about the declining state of my body, I began to compare this visit with my last trip to this institution four or five years ago. A lot has happened at Brookhaven since then: along with remarkable advances in diagnostic medicine, there have been rising costs, shrinking Medicare payments, staff cutbacks, and personnel "realignments." I had talked with nurses and technicians on the picket line, and hospital administrators in their offices. Charlie Rose, the talk show host on PBS, had agreed to narrate a film made by one of my old students, a work that extolled the hospital's preparation for the millennium. The hospital was moving forward or backward, depending on who was talking.

My most recent contact with the hospital had been to cover an emergency drill, held in conjunction with the local fire department. I got to meet the head of the ER services, along with a lot of fine people, and everything ran as smoothly as it did during my own medical crisis five years ago, when the triage unit functioned with almost military precision.

When you visit a place like a hospital, which is the lifeline to the community, comparisons are inevitable. This time around, however, the triage concept seemed to have disappeared. There was one overworked nurse, who was off dealing with a medical emergency of some kind when we staggered through the door. A couple of assistants were with a doctor in a back office, but the waiting room reminded me of the scene from a Fred Wiseman documentary called "Welfare," where a blind man stands in front of an empty desk in a welfare office, waiting for someone to answer his questions.

A pregnant teenager, waiting patiently in a wheel chair, told me to register for my turn by signing a paper on the clipboard sitting on the bottom of the empty window.

The returning nurse deemed that my case, and possibly my gray hairs, qualified me for more immediate care, so my good wife, with the assistance of a couple of gentlemen from Security, managed to get me into a wheel chair. As I was whisked off to the emergency room, the young girl in the other wheel chair gave me a little encouraging wave.

The emergency room staff turned out to be solicitous and efficient, despite the discomfort that is usually experienced there.

After spending four hours in the emergency room, which is, I am told, not bad by today's standards, I was delivered to my quarters on the third floor by a young man who was just beginning his second shift. He had worked the day shift, gone home and had a shower and supper, and returned for a second tour of duty. He said this was a common practice these days, and I reminded him that fewer employees working longer hours seemed to be the custom these days, in education, industry, and government.

A trip to the hospital can be humbling, and enlightening. It's not that we are reminded of our mortality in rude and abrupt ways, but we are also reminded that there are people out there who do not live the sheltered life we enjoy.

My first roommate was a cook from a Chinese restaurant, recently arrived in the United States. He spoke virtually no English, and my Chinese is limited to words found on a menu, so our conversations were rather restricted. When we weren't sleeping (which was most of the time), we managed to get by with a kind of rudimentary sign language. Our goodbyes were formal and polite, as he and his employer bowed their way out the door.

A day passed, and my Asian acquaintance was replaced by the Cisco Kid. The Kid came in with head injuries suffered in a fight, when someone hit him in the head with a two-by-four. He and his girlfriend had been having a party with a kind of extended family who, at one time, had lived in an abandoned theatre. In addition to the Kid's immediate medical problems, their chief concern was where they were going to reside next.

They were looking for an apartment in Holbrook, but the girlfriend was depressed, for their combined financial resources would not meet the requisite deposit. In spite of their myriad problems, they were sweet and gentle and loving with each other. It occurred to me that there were a lot of Cisco Kids on Long Island. We just don't see them, until we go to the hospital.

There followed a series of blood tests, X-rays, CAT scans, as well as the usual routine of IV drips, thermometer readings, and pill presentations administered by a highly professional and competent staff. There was only one problem: in almost every department, the morale seemed to be at rock bottom. A kind of sadness seemed to permeate the nursing and technical staff, a disillusionment that was almost universal.

There was the IV specialist, the only one on duty for the entire hospital, who said that at one time, there had been an IV specialist on every floor. The blood technician echoed her sentiment. Then there was the nurse with more than twenty years of experience, who used to belong to an elite team of floaters who could be utilized in almost every department. She said that group had been disbanded in the staff rearrangement, and the mandated overtime she had been working had almost caused her to have a breakdown. "I can't wait to retire," she said, "and I used to look forward to coming to work."

There are the recently-created multi-purpose aides in their spanking new uniforms, who for a dollar an hour more cleaned rooms, delivered food, and pushed patients in wheel chairs, among other things.

Some of the nurses and technicians I talked to said they were planning to leave for better jobs in the private sector, or hire themselves out on a per diem basis to a number of agencies. They were not angry or militant, just sad that things had changed in a place where "patients" were now called "customers" or "clients."

After all, business is business. By the way, most of the people I talked to did not know that I was a reporter.

The good news is that I was out of the hospital in five days, a few pounds lighter, sadder and wiser, and with a new diet. I had been treated by excellent physicians:and a highly competent surgeon whom I initially mistook for a student aide in her junior year of high school. It turned out she had been a surgeon in the U.S. Navy. I had been cared for by a uniformly professional nursing and technical staff, and everyone else, from housekeeping to food services, was cheerful and polite, in spite of feeling overworked and not entirely happy with things. It would appear that we, the hospital and I, are back on our feet.

On Climbing Mountains

For most of my life, I have been drawn to mountains. Maybe it's because I grew up near the meadowlands of New Jersey, and have spent over half my life living on the south shore of Long Island, where our house is 20 feet above sea level. If global warming becomes a reality, our front lawn will be under water, but I probably won't be around to worry about it.

When my wife and I started traveling to Europe in the Eighties, our trips almost always seemed to involve a mountain or two. On our first trip to France, we wound up in Megeve in the French Alps, with a view of Mont Blanc from our bedroom window. On other trips we visited the Scottish Highlands, Haleakala in Maui, and Mount Etna in Sicily. However, my personal bucket list has always included hiking on the Appalachian Trail, following a string of mountain tops that stretches from Georgia to Maine.

One year I seem to have spent a good part of August climbing mountains.

First there was Mount Graylock, at 3500 feet the highest mountain in Massachusetts and the high point of our annual trek on the Appalachian Trail. While the rest of our crew (one of my sons, our friend Rich, and his son) forged ahead, I huffed and puffed my way to the summit. John, the son of a friend who died about ten years ago, stayed behind to keep me company, which is his way.

This millennium year was a time of superlatives on the Appalachian Trail for thru-hikers: the fastest (a runner, who did the 2,150 miles in 48 days), the youngest (an 11-year-old), and the oldest (a 91-year-older, with strong legs, no doubt.) There are sure to be other records set before the hiking season is over.

On the way up Graylock, John and I talked about his father, Jack, a beloved educator in the local school district, and how, many years ago, he had buried a time capsule on Mount Katahdin, the final peak on the trail in Maine. John hoped that he and his brothers would some day dig up that memento, left by their father before they were born. Knowing John, he will do it.

Rich, who acted as a kind of surrogate father to John on this trip, said, "Jack would be proud of his sons." We agree.

Shortly thereafter, my wife and I found ourselves on top of Cadillac Mountain in Acadia National Park in Maine, and there were the inevitable comparisons. Cadillac is the highest mountain in Acadia, and, as the saying goes, "on a clear day, you can see forever." Like Graylock, there are two ways to get to the summit, by foot and by car. Hikers, after struggling up the long ascent, are greeted by a parking lot full of tourists who have motored their way to the top in air-conditioned comfort, refreshed and deoderized. We walked past one fellow who didn't even get out of his sports utility vehicle, talking on a cell phone to his broker, we presumed, while his wife scampered to the summit on high heels.

It occurred to us that no matter how one gets there, climbing a mountain is an important event in our lives, a kind of metaphysical sticking one's head up and taking a look around. We were also reminded of that old favorite by Robert Frost, "The Road Not Taken," and that it is sometimes better to take the way "less traveled by."

We thought of the long uphill climb the Class of 2000 has to face this year, passing the new Regents exams in order to graduate.

This brings us to another kind of mountain, the pinnacle reached this summer by our friend Sarah, the young woman who was paralyzed from the neck down after a shooting in

North Bellport six years ago. In August, Sarah and her family were moved to a new house in Coram, one that did not have rats, roaches, dubious wiring, and a heating system that only worked on whim. More importantly, Sarah now has a room of her own. In the old house in North Bellport, Sarah's bed could only fit in the living room, and she had no privacy at all. Now she is in a place where she can have the door shut once in awhile, where she can get some sleep.

We went to see Sarah in her new home before our trip to Acadia, and she said, "I feel so much better. I can look out the front window now and see what is going on in the street. I've been sleeping better, too."

The rest has had other salutary effects: Sarah has been able to move her arms a little, and has experienced some sensation in one of her legs. There has been talk of rehabilitation, as Sarah starts to climb her personal mountain.

Good hiking, Sarah.

Of Men and Women

When my neighbor and I went for a hike on the Appalachian Trail, we thought it was going to be a real he-man, macho, Iron John experience. We weren't going to walk the entire 2,150 miles from Maine to Georgia. That was for the real men, the lean, ascetic, tough "Thru-hikers." Twenty or thirty miles in the relatively gentle Berkshires was enough for a couple of sedentary suburbanites. We spent half a year in the planning, talking guy talk, making forays to the local outdoor camping store, poring over the latest issues of the L.L. Bean catalogue. I started riding my bike around the block with more regularity, and thought about lifting weights.

Little did we know that the experience was going to bring out the feminine side of our nature.

We set out from Cornwall Bridge in Connecticut on a hot day in the middle of July. We were six strong: my neighbor and his son, my son, a mutual friend who was something of a naturalist, and the two fatherless sons of another friend who had died too soon to go hiking with his boys. An all-male cast of characters.

As we made our way along the trail, we began to take on (forgive me, feminist wife) womanish roles. One of the boys had a torn sleeping bag, so we had to break out the sewing kit and repair it. I was the designated cook, planning menus and crouching over a propane stove to prepare breakfast and dinner. (Open fires are not permitted on the trail in Connecticut and Massachusetts.) Lunch consisted of trail mix, beef jerky, and that old standby, the peanut butter and grape jelly sandwich. Two of the boys became housekeepers and dishwashers, and one was in charge of treating the water with chemicals. My neighbor, an EMT, was our resident nurse, tending to cuts, blisters, and bruises.

More than taking on jobs that admittedly could be done by men and women equally, there was the spirit of cooperation that prevailed. The notion of competition, that ethic that had dominated our male upbringing and ruled our lives, was noticeably absent from our daily trek. We helped each other with heavy backpacks, warned the following hikers about a difficult stretch of terrain, gave each other a hand with a steep climb. As the oldest and least physically fit member of the group, I gratefully accepted offers from the younger campers to lighten my load a bit.

I was really struggling on a particularly difficult nine-mile hike through the drought-stricken mountains of northwestern Connecticut, and on that afternoon, one of the young men not only conceived a plan to help me out, but did so with tact and grace and sensitivity. He said, "Here, you wait with my pack while I carry yours ahead a bit. Then I'll come back and we can go on." He did this twice, carrying two packs and allowing me to rest my 62-year-old bones. On that afternoon, the fatherless son became his father, because that's the kind of thing Jack would have done.

The most feminine aspect of the trail was the talk. Men do not chat, men do confrontational guy talk, arguing about baseball, weather, cars.

Deborah Tannen, Professor of Linguistics and author of *You Just Don't Understand: Men and Women in Conversation,* says, in effect, that men talk to give reports, to preserve independence, to hold center stage, while women talk to achieve rapport, to establish connections, and negotiate relationships. She may have a point. When I talk on the telephone, it is mostly to give or get information, then hang up.

On the trail maybe the complete absence of electronic devices and distractions unleashed torrents of talk. We chatted, we gossiped, we schmoozed, we told stories. My neighbor and I talked more in one day than we had in an entire year.

And we did not talk baseball or cars. We spoke of love, of death, of desire and fears. We talked about the past and the future. Serious, heady stuff.

The boys picked up on our lead. They were not as verbose during the day, but we could hear them chattering into the night in their tent.

After hiking over 21 miles, a hundredth of the length of the trail, we decided to call it quits for this year. The drought was too severe. All the creeks and streams, valuable sources of needed water, had dried up, and the hike had become an exercise in survival.

As we packed our gear into the van, we swore to pick up next year where we had left off. Maybe one of these days we or our young companions would see the slopes of Mount Katahdin in Maine. For me, the process was the important thing. The planning and the doing. Most important, as I think of it, was the rapport talk, and the chance to be a complete human being.

A Postcard from the Appalachian Trail

"Why?" my wife asked, as my neighbor and I prepared for our third annual hike on the Appalachian Trail.

"Why, indeed," I thought to myself, as I mentally prepared for a week of sleeping on the ground, sore feet, aching muscles. Was it some kind of "Iron John" thing, an atavistic yearning to get back to nature, to tear off the shackles of wimpdom for at least one week a year? I tried to reassure my wife that our annual adventure was not such an exercise, but I don't think she believed me.

There were four of us: Rich, my neighbor, lean and fit after another season of coaching tennis at the local high school; his son Dave, who finished high in the county tennis standings this year; my youngest son Ted, an off-road biker; and your faithful correspondent.

Another young man from Bellport, a stalwart in our first two ventures, was supposed to have gone with us, but called at the last minute, saying he couldn't miss any time from work, that college expenses loomed in the fall. This news sent our group into a swamp of self-doubt. Did our sons really want to go, or were they going because we wanted them to? My neighbor's back started acting up; his son had been invited to numerous graduation parties; my son complained of a sore back too, perhaps in anticipation of carrying a forty-pound pack. Who would drop out next?

My spirits lifted when my son came home with a sleeping pad and a huge Bowie-type survival knife. As we packed, he and I talked more than we had for the last month. We weighed and re-weighed the packs, finally arriving at 35 pounds for my son, and 30 for me, in deference to my age.

The next day, we arrived in Salisbury, Connecticut, where we had left the trail two years ago due to a severe drought. There has been a lot of rain this year, and we were optimistic about finding water in the mountains. In spite of a steep climb, we made it to the summit of Lion's Head (1,738 feet) in about three hours and continued on about a mile to our first campsite. On our way there, we met an ATC (Appalachian Trail Conference) "Ridgerunner," a college student hired for the summer to patrol the trail, helping hikers and delivering two admonishments heard from Georgia to Maine: "No fires" (in certain states) and, "Stay on the Trail." There are cases where lone hikers have left the trail, become injured, and not found for days or weeks.

Properly warned, we sat down to a sumptuous meal of Spam, mashed potatoes, and freeze-dried vegetables. After supper, we took stock: my neighbor had back spasms, his son had developed a blister, my son had a sore back, and my 64-year-old legs were shouting, "What, are you crazy?"

Things were not looking good, but after a cool night's sleep and a little breakfast of cereal and Tang, we pushed on.

The first topic of trail talk for the day was the idea of zero population growth. We started by talking about families we knew who have five or more children, then the conversation led to global applications. Then we talked about the book *Blind Courage,* and wondered how author Bill Irwin, who was blind, managed the roots and rocks that make the simplest path a treacherous passage.

We hiked too long on the second day, caught up in trail conversation and the panoramic views from Bear and Race Mountains. My son put a sprig of mountain laurel in his hat, and I sensed he was beginning to enjoy the outing.

During lunch, we talked about roles. My neighbor's son was dubbed the Pathfinder, for his uncanny ability to follow the trail. My neighbor was the Medicine Man, for he is an EMT with the local ambulance company. My son was named the Artist, doing a lot of wood carving with his new knife, and they elected me as the Shaman, probably because I am the oldest hiker in our group, and I do most of the cooking, crouched over a propane burner.

We had trouble finding a decent campsite, as the stream had dried up and there was no water available. We hiked downstream, and eventually found a suitable place. It was late in the day, for we had hiked almost nine miles, up and down several mountains. My son was suffering from heat exhaustion and dehydration, and I had twisted my ankle, joining the list of the walking wounded. A little voice in my ear whispered, "I told you so."

The next morning, it was decision time: to hike two miles down the mountain on a side trail and hitch a ride back to the car, or to struggle on. My son seemed to have recovered; in fact, he sat up half the night with my neighbor's son, talking over a campfire (we had reached Massachusetts, where such things are permitted). My ankle was tender, but once into a stout hiking boot, seemed to be all right. We dawdled over breakfast, then decided to push onward and literally upward on a one-mile, very steep ascent of Mount Everitt, at 2,602 feet the highest mountain on this trip. The view at the summit was magnificent: to the north was Monument Mountain, to the northeast, Mount Graylock, the highest in Massachusetts, and in the distance to the west were the Catskills. On the way up, the sight of a couple of eastern garter snakes had given us a frisson, as we had been reading about the endangered timber rattlesnake the night before.

We headed down off Mount Everitt to Guilder Pond, the second highest pond in the state, where we had a delightful lunch of Oriental noodles and pita bread in a picnic area near a mountain road leading to a fire tower. The warm soup and salt seemed to restore us, and our spirits became further revived by the appearance of two comely young women on a Suzuki motorcycle. After exchanging pleasantries, they went off down to the pond for a swim. Our sons immediately volunteered to wash the cooking utensils in the pond.

After a short nap, my neighbor and I headed down to to see what had become of our sons. We joined them and the young women on a large rock, where we went for a refreshing swim. It turned out that the women had been thru-hikers last year, taking six months off to trek the full 2,150 plus (the trail has recently been extended to the north) miles from Georgia to Maine. We were suitably impressed.

As we headed back to our packs and resumed our hike, we all agreed that in spite of our various ailments, things were beginning to look brighter. We reached our intended campsite, which turned out to have a dried-up creek. Our sons volunteered to hike down an ancillary trail to find water, and within the hour, our faithful bearers had returned with enough water to get us through the night and into the next day. That night, facing the toughest descent of the trip, we had a feast: freeze-dried turkey risotto, red beans and rice, tamale pie, and noodles, washed down with Tang, Tia Maria, and port wine, with Tootsie Rolls for dessert. Running low on food, we had just enough for one more day of extended hiking.

After a 2.8-mile steep descent of Jug End, we were out of water, but we found a roadside spring fed by an artesian well that had the clearest, coldest water to be found on the trip.

As we hiked six miles across the Housatonic River Valley, through white pine forests and verdant fields and pastures, traversing ancient stone walls and bog bridges, making our way towards the historical marker commemorating Daniel Shay's Rebellion of 1787, I thought of my wife's question. I thought about being away from faxes, e-mail, voice mail. I thought about real space reasserting itself, banishing cyberspace to its rightful perspective. I thought about reconnecting with my youngest son. Finally, I was reminded that hiking reduces "life to its simplest elements," as that old wanderer Thoreau said. Walking, cooking, eating, setting up shelter for the night, carrying everything with us, including our garbage. The air is pure. The only sound is our breathing after a hard climb, the trill of a songbird in a nearby tree, and the talk, the glorious talk that flows when there are no television sets, radios, newspapers, and magazines to tell us what to think.

Another Postcard from the Trail

I was not a happy camper this year. We had to delay our annual hike on the Appalachian Trail by one day so that one member of our party could return from Maine. As if that were not bad enough, on the first day out we learned that he had to be back a day early to go back to work.

This news came shortly after I had removed my watch.

Suddenly what was intended to be a pleasant walk in the woods became a race against time, a headlong rush over rocks and roots to cover five days' hiking in four.

The thing is that when you're 65, twenty pounds heavier than you should be, and carrying a pack that weighs at least 30 pounds, you tend to know your limitations. I figured with the hills and mountains and rock slides, I could average about five to six miles a day. We covered over 30 miles in four days.

I tried to compensate for my mile-an-hour walking speed by setting out each day an hour ahead of our group. Sure enough, in about an hour, they would pass me, and I would spend the rest of the day huffing and puffing to catch up.

However, the defining moment of the trip for me took place as I was struggling to the summit of Baldy Mountain, when my son came back down the trail and relieved me of my pack. It's a memory I will cherish.

There were other mental snapshots worth saving: spending a rainy night in a shelter with some thru-hikers (yes, that's how it's spelled, as in New York Thruway) eager for news, any news, even the latest tawdry developments in Washington; waking to 40-degree temperatures and hearing the first bird call of the morning; eating lunch on a ledge overlooking a series of mountains; finding a cold, clear spring with pristine water; finally reaching the Trail bridge across the Massachusetts

Turnpike and becoming one of those hikers I had dreamed about in past years as we drove underneath on our way to Lenox.

Each year our hike seems to have its own special quality. One year, it was unrelenting drought, when the streams dried out and we had to cut our trip short. Last year, our trek was characterized by magnificent views from the tops of Race Mountain and Mount Everitt. This year seemed to be marked by people, mostly thru-hikers. We seemed to be traveling through Massachusetts when the last wave of south-to-north and north-to-south thru-hikers were passing through. These particular hikers, rugged individuals who are going the whole 2,150-mile route, from Mount Katahdin in the central Maine woods to Springer Mountain in Georgia, travel light and fast, and rarely stop to enjoy the view. The object is to get there.

This special fraternity (and sorority) that hikes the full distance constitutes about one percent of all those who walk on the trail. They give themselves special nicknames: Mouse, Sky Walker, Pokey, The Illustrated Man, Star Burst, and Happy Feet. And then there was Earl Shaffer.

On our first night in the shelter, the thru-hikers spoke in hushed and respectful terms of the legendary Earl Shaffer, the first man to walk the entire length of the Appalachian Trail by himself, as if he were a figure from Greek mythology. This year, at the age of 80, Shaffer was celebrating the fiftieth anniversary of that initial feat by doing it again.

"Did you hear? Earl's on the trail again."

"Yeah, I heard he was giving an interview to the media over in Egremont."

"Do you think we'll see him?"

On the third night out, just as the sun was setting, a spectral figure strolled by our campsite. He paused, then moved on. The boys called out to him, but he didn't seem to take notice.

Later, we were to find out that the ghostly apparition was Earl Shaffer himself.

We caught up with him the next day, just as we were about to finish our hike. He didn't look like a legend: wisps of grey hair under a pith helmet with mosquito netting, an old frayed plaid shirt, work boots with no socks, an old army-surplus rucksack. As we walked across the turnpike bridge together, he remarked that he was low on food (peanut butter and bread), so we volunteered to drive him into the nearby village of Lee for provisions when we picked up our van. While he was shopping, we invited him to join us for breakfast, and over eggs, steak, and hash-browned potatoes, he told us that this would be his last hike.

"I'm slowing down," he said. He said that he didn't carry a tent, just a couple of tarps. "I just like to sleep on the top of a mountain," said the 80-year-old from Idaville, Pennsylvania. Shaffer had two physical examination—his first since leaving the army 50 years ago—to prepare for the trip. "The doctors couldn't find anything wrong with me," he said.

He said that when he made his first journey, the trail was not as well maintained, and harder to find. A lot of his walking took place on roads. "One thing that makes it harder now is the erosion," he said, "the exposed rocks and tree roots are harder on the feet."

Shaffer wrote a book about his first hiking adventure, called *Walking with Spring*, published in 1983. In a 1949 article, *National Geographic* cited Shaffer as the first to make the entire trip alone, and he was recently featured in a television news special about the Trail. However, he says he's really not interested in getting a lot of notice. He described himself as a "jack of all trades," having worked as a farmer, beekeeper, and construction worker. He never married, and feels the key to staying healthy was to not smoke and drink.

We left Earl Shaffer at the trail head on the way to October Mountain, bent under the weight of his forty-pound pack but not his age, and returned to Long Island and the worst Friday afternoon traffic mess in years.

The thought of this venerable trekker reminds us of a quote by Henry David Thoreau, who walked these parts himself some years ago: "If a man does not keep pace with his companions, perhaps it is because he hears a different drummer. Let him step to the music which he hears, however measured or far away."

Perhaps Thoreau, and Earl Shaffer, can teach us all a valuable lesson about hiking—and life.

Postcard from Spain

Somewhere over the Atlantic: Well, here we are, on our way to Spain at last. Sunny Spain: the land of Ferdinand the Bull, Hemingway, El Greco, Velasquez, Cervantes, and Garcia Lorca. Spanish castles, El Cid, the rain in Spain doesn't fall anywhere near the plain, at least for much of spring and summer, we're told. Spain: flamenco dancers, sherry, olives, Washington Irving's Alhambra. Living there for three months in 1829, he looked out from his apartment in the Generalife Gardens at the snow-capped Sierra Nevada and wrote: "The Moors imagined that the celestial paradise hung over this favored spot." Later, in the light of a full moon, he asked, "Who can do justice to a moonlit night in such a climate and such a place?" Who indeed.

Here's what we will be doing for the next three weeks. Hopefully, we will send you another postcard from time to time, to let you know how we are getting along.

When we get to Madrid tomorrow night, we plan to spend several days decompressing from the eight-hour flight and exploring the city, adjusting to the language, seeing if months of listening to Spanish tapes pays off. We enter the country with some trepidation: it seems that everyone who has been to Spain has a horror story about being ripped off, mugged, having a bag stolen or a purse snatched. Having successfully fought off or avoided gypsies and street urchins in France and Italy, we remind ourselves that one has to be careful in countries that have little welfare support, that there are probably as many pickpockets in Paris as there are in all of Spain. Forewarned is forearmed, they say.

After a couple of days in Madrid, we plan to take a fast train to Seville, fourth largest city in Spain and featured in last Sunday's *New York Times* Travel Section, we were happy to see. We look forward to the whitewashed houses bright with bougainvillea, ocher palaces, baroque facades described in the article. We do not look forward to the traffic-choked streets, the city's reputation for petty crime, and plan to stay there for only one day before renting a car and heading farther south.

We plan to drive to Gibraltar, leave the car at Algecieras, and take the ferry to Tangiers, Morocco, where we will spend two nights in the Hotel Continental, an Old World palace built in 1888 that overlooks the port from the edge of the medina. Through the hotel, we hope to engage the services of a reliable guide who will take us to the Fondouk Market.

After taking the ferry back to Algecieras, we will drive to Malaga, where we will stay in a parador, a government-owned and operated hotel, usually based in an old castle or historic building. The parador in Malaga is surrounded by pine trees on top of Gibralfaro Mountain, two miles above the city, built of gray stone and smothered in ivy. The views of the city and the bay are reported to be spectacular.

Leaving Malaga after a couple of days, we will drive to Granada, home of the Alhambra, gypsy caves, and the old Moorish quarter. We plan to drop off the rental car there, and explore most of the city on foot.

After three days in Granada, we plan to take a flight to Valencia and soak up some Spanish history. The city's location, on a fertile plain, has been fiercely contested ever since its foundation by the Greeks. If anyone remembers the Charlton Heston movie, this is the city that El Cid captured from the Moors in 1094 and won his strangest victory there in 1099, when his corpse was strapped to his saddle, causing a complete rout among the frightened Moors.

A day or so in Valencia, then up the eastern coast by train to Barcelona, supposedly one of the most beautiful and modern cities in Europe. A vibrant city with its own Catalan identity, Barcelona has been home to the likes of Picasso, Miro, and Dali, as well as the 1992 Olympics, which signaled its rebirth as a modern city.

After a few days in Barcelona, we will get on the train once again, and head for Madrid and the bullfights, as well as side trips to Toledo, a historic gem, and medieval Avila, the home of St. Teresa.

From time to time, we'll let you know how things are going. *Hasta la vista.*

What Really Happened on Our Trip to Spain

At first our trip to Spain went pretty much as expected. However, there were a few unexpected things worth talking about.

When we got to Madrid, the city appeared empty. When the cab dropped us off in front of our hotel, the street was deserted. It was about 9:00 p.m., around the time when folks there think about going to the tapas bars and dinner. When we entered the hotel, I saw a bar just off the lobby, packed with intense football (soccer) fans. It turned out that Spain was in the semi-finals of the World Cup, and everybody in Madrid was glued to a television set somewhere. About an hour later, fans erupted into the streets, screaming, blowing horns, waving flags. Spain was on its way to the finals. Not much sleep that night.

We took a train to Seville, and got our first taste of the flamenco. Renting a car, we headed farther south, winding up in the port town of Algiceras. It was raining when we arrived, and I saw a ferry preparing to leave. We parked the car in a lot and ran for the ferry, paying for our tickets on the fly. We thought the ferry was headed for Tangiers, Morocco. The crossing seemed very brief, and when the ship arrived in a port, we prepared to get off. The official who took out tickets greeted us with, "Sorry, this is not Tangiers. You have arrived in Spanish Ceutas."

I said to the official, "But we wanted to go to Tangiers."

He replied with a patient smile, as if dealing with ignorant Americans was something he did every day, "Well, senor, if you can get across the border, you can take a taxi to Tangiers. It is just on the other side of the mountains."

We went to a money exchange, and cashed in some dollars for something called "dirham," the money used in Morocco. The propietor of the money exchange told us if we were going to Tangiers we should engage the services of an expeditor, in fact, his cousin, who for the paltry sum of 300 dirham would help us get through customs and border officials.

As we were led across the border into Morocco, we looked at the armed guards and harried looking refugees huddled on the side of the road. It turned out that the political situation in Morocco was a bit unstable at the time, and Spanish officials were hard pressed from keeping refugees out of Ceutas.

When we got to the Morocco side of the border, our guide said, "You want to go to Tangiers, yes?"

When we agreed, he said, "I have a cousin, he will take you to Tangiers for 300 dirham."

We agreed, and followed our guide to a row of ancient Mercedes sedans. After a heated discussion, our guide handed us over to a taxi driver, who kicked an old lady out of the front of the sedan.

"Who is that?" I asked our guide.

He said, "Oh, that is his mother. She will wait for him here until he returns."

So off we went, in a cloud of dust and diesel exhaust fumes, up and over the Atlas Mountains. In many places, the road was washed out, and we had to take a detour. The circuitous route took us throught many small towns, and at each case, we had to stop at the local police station, where the driver would present our passports and a few dirham.

We asked the driver why he had to make so many stops, but he just shrugged his shoulders and said, "For securite, you know. There are a lot of terrorists about." His English was not much better than my high school French, so we lapsed into long periods of silence, watching the peasants as they drove their heavily-laden donkeys toward town.

After an eight-hour ride, we pulled up to the outer limits of Tangiers. Our driver stopped the car, and he held the door open for us with one hand, and the other extended for payment.

I said, "Wait. We want to go to the port of Tangiers. This is the other side of town."

The cab driver shrugged, then said, "I take you to Tangiers. This is Tangiers. I do not have permit to drive in the city."

Then he relented, and said, "I will call you Tangiers taxi."

About a half an hour later, another taxi appeared in a cloud of dust. A few more dirham exchanged hands, and our first driver left, no doubt on his way back to the border and his mother.

Our new driver, a lean fellow with a mouthful of broken and missing teeth, said "Where you going?"

I named our destination, the Hotel Continental.

Entering the hotel, we realized that the place had seen better days. The rugs were frayed, the table tops were dusty, and there was a general air of decay about the place. Our rooms were on the top floor, with a great view of the city, its mosques, and the port. That was about all it had going for it, however. When we looked at the lumpy mattresses, the torn and stained sheets, and the cockroaches scurrying about the bathroom, we decided we would be staying for only one night.

The next day, we rushed down the hill to the ferry terminal and caught the next boat to Algeceris. After getting our rental car out of the parking lot, we drove to Gibralter for lunch, then headed for Malaga, a bustling port on the Mediterranean. We found our way to a parador overlooking the bull ring in that city, and stayed in the swimming pool for an hour or so before dinner, soaking away the grime of travel and bad memories of Tangiers.

Leaving Malaga the next day, clean and refreshed, we headed for Granada and the Alhambra, to stay in another parador, a state-run elegant hotel. The next day, we drove to the Granada Airport, planning to fly to Barcelona. After turning in the rental car, we headed for the terminal, only to find that there were no flights, due to an air traffic controllers' strike. We rushed back to the rental lot, and were lucky enough to retrieve our car. There followed a long, tortuous drive up the southwestern coast of Spain to Valencia, where we once again returned our car and took the train to Barcelona. The trip took two days instead of the planned two hours. It doesn't look like it on a school map, but Spain is a very big country.

Postcard from Sainte Maxime, France

After a week of reacquainting ourselves with the pleasures of Paris, we were ready for the Cote d'Azur, drawn to the incredible light and fresh air that attracted Matisse and many other French painters in the 19th century.

We took the TGV, a high-speed train, to Toulon, a port city generally dismissed by travel writers. Staying in a delightful little hotel overlooking the picturesque harbor, we decided that Toulon was one of those chance discoveries that make unescorted travel so much fun.

The next day, we took a cab, then a ferry to the Ile de Porquerolles, an island off the coast that is mostly a nature preserve. Like Fire Island, no cars were allowed on the island, and if one wanted to travel outside the little seaside village, there were bikes for hire. The island, enjoyed by nude bathers and sailors alike, was a welcome break after the hustle and bustle of Paris, and after a few days, we felt ready for our mission to Sainte Maxime.

Finding out that we were traveling to our home town's sister city, the mayor had asked us to take a village flag and a few other tokens of good will to the mayor of Sainte Maxime.

Leaving the island of Porquerelles with some regret, we took a cab to the airport in Hyeres, where we rented a car. As it so often happens on our travels, we took the wrong road, a torturous, single-lane roller coaster ride through the foothills of Provence with no shoulders and no guard rails, leaving little opportunity to enjoy the scenery.

Reaching Sainte Maxime with some relief, we signed into the Hotel Belle Aurore, which lived up to its name since it is the only hotel on the waterfront, with spacious beaches on either side and an excellent view. We sat down to lunch and watched brightly adorned sailboats dancing across the water, as well as the ferry that crossed the bay to Saint Tropez.

The next day, we climbed the imposing steps to the Hotel de Ville. The city hall looked very little like its stateside counterpart: the three-story museum-like edifice looking out over a thriving town was surrounded by spacious gardens and fountains. Shortly after our arrival, the mayor, dressed in tie and jacket, pulled up on a motor scooter. The mayor spoke no English, so we struggled along in our rudimentary high school French until the mayor's assistant, who had been educated in England, showed up. We were also joined by the commandant des sapeurs-pompiers (the fire chief), who spoke a little English.

After exchanging gifts and felicitations, the mayor put on his official sash and went off to marry a couple on the next floor. Meanwhile, with the help of the assistant, we had a long discussion with the chief about firefighting in the area. It turns out that the south of Provence has many of the same problems that we have, specifically brush fires (feu de foret) in the hot, dry summer months and a dire need for more volunteers. Also, in the high season, the town is inundated by traffic, just as we were in our home town.

Afterward, my wife went back to the hotel to watch the yachts racing in the bay, and the chief took me on a tour of the city firehouse, culminating in a number of toasts with glasses of pastis, a lethal drink from Provence, and pledges of lifelong friendship.

Returning to the hotel, I made a promise to myself: never drink in the afternoon, especially if it's pastis in a French firehouse.

In the Age of Innocence: Birdsall Otis Edey

Imagine a wedding in Bellport at the turn of the 19th Century, the age of innocence, as it might be described by Edith Wharton.

It is almost noon at "Nearthebay," the palatial home of former Senator James Otis. The gardeners have trimmed the house with flowers and vines, as the servants set out tables with fine linen, crystal ware, and silver service. White-gloved liverymen in top hats open the doors of horse-drawn carriages that have come up the long drive to the mansion, bringing guests who have just arrived on a special train from New York engaged for the occasion.

The Senator, having spent most of the previous week sailing and fishing "out of the way of the womenfolk" on his big, single-sailed catboat on the bay, has donned his tuxedo and greets the guests with a jolly, sunburned face, his broad shoulders shaking at the latest joke by a fishing crony.

Upstairs, his daughter, Sarah Birdsall Otis, stands before a mirror as her attendants put the finishing touches on a white satin dress finished with fine, old lace, most of which has been in the family for years. No doubt, her mind is occupied with thoughts of the man she is about to marry, whom she met five years earlier on a cruise to Europe.

The bridegroom, popular society and clubman Frederick Edey, arrived the day before from his residence on West 46th Street. It is said that it took the popular stockbroker a full half hour to get through the gantlet of well-wishers from his office at Broad and Wall Streets to another office a block away. Edey was a member of the New York Union, the Union League, and the prestigious Manhattan Club.

On his wedding day, Edey stands in a large living room at NeartheBay, just off the spacious foyer, smoking a cigar with several politicians and captains of industry. While it is September, fires have been lit in the marble fireplaces in all of the rooms to take the morning chill out of the air.

In the basement rooms, including the kitchen, servants rush to and fro, preparing the wedding feast and bringing drinks from the wine cellar to the guests.

The house, built by Henry Weeks Titus in 1835, was purchased in 1865 by James Otis, who lived nearby. A gentleman farmer for nearly twenty years, Otis, who was elected state senator in 1883, had raised cattle, sheep, and hogs, and grown wheat, corn, barely, and rye on the Otis family estate that was part of Old Purchase South called "Starr's Neck," over two hundred acres reaching from what is now South Country Road to Great South Bay from north to south, and from Academy Lane in the east to Lyman Road in the west. Part of this estate is now the Bellport Country Club and Golf Course. Even in those days, great piles of seaweed were harvested from the beach and used as compost.

In the future, the house would become the property of the Senator's daughter, Birdsall Otis Edey, when she inherited his estate and lived there and at her New York residence until her death in 1940. It would be the birthplace of her daughter, the late Julia Paige, and her grandson, the late Peter Paige, who was to become the personnel director of Brookhaven National Laboratory and chairman of the board of directors of Brookhaven Memorial Hospital. Before his passing, he lived in retirement with his wife, the late Natalie Paige, on nearby Gerard Lane.

The west wing of Nearthebay would be moved by barge to Titus Lane in Bellport, becoming the home of the late Charles and Sheila Paige Dominy, Mrs. Edey's granddaughter.

The last owners of the estate would be Mr. and Mrs. Leslie Weiss. Weiss was the president of PELCO, the Patchogue Electric Company. It is said that Mrs. Weiss refused to have electricity in the dining room, as she preferred to dine by candle light. After the death of the Weisses, the house would be restored to its former glory by "Here Comes the Sun," a local contracting company dedicated to saving the stately mansion from the brink of destruction. Where there was once gaslight, new electric, plumbing, heating, and alarm systems were installed. A new kitchen appeared on the first floor, and the detailed wood floors were refinished.

However, this story is not just about a house; it's about the bride, Birdsall, or as she preferred to be called by family and friends, "Bird" Otis Edey, an extraordinary woman who lived a Charles Dana Gibson life of beautiful women and handsome men playing croquet at tea parties, but also used her wealth and position to serve humanity.

Beginning with Bellport, where she drove one of the first automobiles in the village, Bird Edey helped finance the village's first golf course, sat on the library board, fought to save the fine old trees from those who wanted to widen the streets, and succeeded in getting the state highway to pass by a half a mile to the north. Under her presidency, the Bellport Village Improvement Society raised funds for lamp posts and provided for lighting the streets at night, watered the dusty streets in the summer, and effected the extension of Bellport Lane to the bay. The ivy-covered playhouse she had built for her daughter and her friends became a center for such activities as children's theatricals, benefit performances for such causes as women's suffrage, or a meeting to consider improvements to the nearby Episcopal Church. A few old-timers remember the presentation of "The Prune Hater's Daughter," or "More Sinned Against Than Usual."

In the days before women's suffrage, Bird Otis Edey campaigned to get the vote for women. When that objective was accomplished, she turned her attention to the Girl Scouts, eschewing politics. She wrote: "I decided it would be more useful to me to help train a new generation of women who would be good citizens."

Bird Edey had joined the Girl Scout movement in 1918, when the organization was almost six years old. While helping a Girl Scout troop to sell war bonds to crowds on Wall Street in 1919, she was impressed by the young girls who worked by her side, and further touched when three of the girls visited her in the hospital with flowers they had gathered on a hike.

Sometime later, Juliette Gordon Low, the founder of the Girl Scouts with whom Bird was to develop a lifelong friendship, approached her to present badges at an awards ceremony, and that request signaled the beginning of a permanent involvement with the Girl Scout movement.

Bird Edey's first post was as Commissioner of the Manhattan Council of Girl Scouts in 1919, and by the next year she was elected to the National Board of Directors, appointed chairman of the National Field Committee, and became a member of the Executive Committee. As chairman of the National Field Committee, an appointment that lasted from 1920 until 1930, she traveled around the country organizing Girl Scout operations and defending the emerging individualism of young women everywhere.

She was one of the few Girl Scout leaders who could go into a town and organized a troop on the spot. A tall woman of regal stature, Edey was described as an extraordinary speaker who loved to tell stories, recite and compose poetry, play games, perform folk dances, and engage in humorous songs after a long day of camping. Known by her admirers as "Ma Field," Edey defended the flappers of the Roaring Twenties, saying, "The girl of today is reliable and full of energy. She is capable in meeting situations that the older generation knew nothing about, and she is far more responsible than her elders were."

In 1935, when Mrs. Herbert Hoover was elected national president of the Girl Scouts, the organization created the office of national commissioner for Bird Edey. In addition, Edey became a member of the national finance and personnel committees, as well as chairman of the international committee until her death in 1940 at the age of 67. In 1937 Bird Edey arranged the Girl Scouts' Silver Jubilee observance, and just prior to her death, had completed plans for an encampment of Girl Scouts and Girl Guides from 15 countries. For many years, Camp Edey in Bayport bore her name.

In addition to her 21 years of service to Girl Scouting, Bird Edey wrote a book of short stories for children, *Six Giants and a Griffin,* and three books of poetry: *Rivets*, published in 1928; *Butter Money*, dedicated to the Girl Scouts and published in 1931; and *Builders,* published in 1940, which contains poems to Juliette Low and the Girl Scouts. Bird Edey served as president of the New York Chapter of the League of American Pen Women, the Craftsman Group for Poetry, and the South Shore Women's Club of Long Island.

One of the poems in her book *Builders* was written for her grandson, the late Peter Paige. Called "A Grandmother's Prayer, in a School Chapel," and it goes as follows:

God, bless these manly little heads, black, brown, and fair,
That bow so confidently. Hear the prayer
That comes from young hearts free of all care.
God, bless these noisy feet that clatter to Thy door
So trustingly, and may these boys come more and more
To thee for wisdom from thy never-ending store.
Prolong their singing years, I humbly pray,
Teach them the truth, give them the strength to say
"Thy will be done," and mean it every day.
And that one who is mine, teach him to see
The right, to face life without fear, to be
Considerate, and then…take care of him for me.

Her late grandson's family has flourished, with three
sons growing up in Bellport. At last report, there were seven
grandchildren. It would appear that Birdsall Otis Edey's prayer
has been answered.

The Tap Dance Kid

There's a noisy revolution going on in Suffolk County, punctuated by shouts of boisterous lines of tap dancers and the sounds of metal hitting the hardwood floors.

A few years ago, there was a charming little film called *The Tap Dance Kid,* featuring a talented, six-year-old terpsichorean who could dance as well as Mr. Bojangles himself. So when my wife asked me if I was interested in signing up with her for tap dancing lessons at the Stage Door School of Dance, I said to myself, "Why not? I can do this." My wife, who had studied tap dancing as a youngster, reassured me that the lessons would be good exercise, another way to fight that package that seemed to have attached itself to my waistline in the last year or so. I had visions of becoming a geriatric Michael Flatley, starring in a senior citizen version of "Riverdance," or another Gene Kelly, who danced well into his sixties, with my spouse as Cyd Charisse.

My wife took my old pair of loafers to Jimmy's Shoe Repair in Patchogue. For a nominal fee, Jimmy attached a set of taps to my shoes, and I must admit to a tingle of secret pleasure when I tried them on in the store. That sexy, sensuous sound brought back the Forties and Fifties of my youth, when bad boys like James Dean and Sal Mineo clicked their way through the halls of high schools across the country, thrilling girls in full skirts and enraging school administrators dedicated to stamping out tight pants and ducktail haircuts.

Then reality set it. As a boy in Northern New Jersey, I had failed at any attempts to learn how to dance, for I seemed to have been born with two left feet. Moreover, I have always been a little dyslexic. To make things worse, Diane Giattino, the instructor and owner of Stage Door, told us that we always start on the right foot, and I am left-handed. In the dance studio, my confusion was compounded when I found myself looking in a full-length mirror that covered a complete wall. Which was left, and which was right? Help!

Diane was the epitome of patience as she led us through some warm-up exercises. I looked around at the other dancers: Donna and Lorraine, a daughter and mother team; Roberta, who is recovering from heart surgery; Marie, mother of three in the middle of chemotherapy; Patty, the florist from next door; and a couple of nurses from nearby Brookhaven Memorial Hospital. We are a mixed group, indeed. The fact that I am the only male in the class, and a rather clumsy one at that, is a little disconcerting, but the ladies are gentle with me.

Diane, who learned her trade for 25 cents a lesson in a Bronx Catholic school gym, has been running the school in East Patchogue for the last 24 years. She told me that a few years ago she had an all-male tap dance class, comprised of a police detective, a priest, a couple of firemen, and some construction workers. She said, "The class lasted about 16 months, then everybody's work schedule got in the way." She can't fool me. The guys probably quit when they found out she was planning to put them in her annual recital, a cast of thousands appearing in the Staller Center at Stony Brook.

Presently, there are over 500 students, ranging from age 2 to 66, attending various classes at the Stage Door School of Dance. Figure an average of two parents and four grandparents per child, plus assorted siblings and friends, and it's easy to see why last year's spring recital had to be spread over three days.

Many of the instructors have professional credentials: Melissa Giattino, Diane's daughter, was a Rockette for three years and toured with national companies of Peter Pan, Chorus Line, 42nd Street, and the London production of Showboat;

ballet teacher Pat Monaco danced with Mikhail Baryshnikov in The Nutcracker Suite with the American Ballet Company, and appeared with him in the movie "The Turning Point;" Kelly Barclay performed in Broadway shows, and was the assistant choreographer at Radio City Music Hall; Colleen Murphy, Shelley Herbert, and Christine Cierello majored in dance at their respective colleges; Marissa Rignola, Miss Teen NY State in 1994, has appeared as a dancer on MTV; and Rick Kerby performed and choreographed national touring shows and performed at the Aladdin in Las Vegas.

I also learned that many former students have gone on to careers on and off Broadway. The latest alumni success stories are Missy Sybil and Kristen Armann, Rockette and ballet dancer respectively who are currently appearing at Radio City Music Hall.

Gotta dance!

The warm-up in our first class is a piece of cake: brush, step, stop, brush, step, stop; slap, slapstep, ball change. Things begin to get a bit complicated. I feel like a ninth grader back in Northern New Jersey, trying to master the foxtrot in Mrs. Vollmer's dance class, hoping my partner would not notice the zit on the end of my nose.

As we execute a couple of turns across the floor, I fail to find my mark, and suddenly the room begins to spin. I get the feeling that my classmates are standing there with arms crossed, tapping their shoes as they wait for me to get it right. However, when I finally stagger to the other side of the room, they burst into applause, either out of relief or from exasperation, I'm not sure, but Diane assures me that it is in appreciation for my efforts.

Suddenly my legs begin cramping up, protesting that they have never been abused in exactly this fashion before. I am sweating, as if I have just finished hiking for ten miles. I look in the mirror: Who is this fat old guy huffing and puffing his way through some impossible routine ? If my children, who are grown men, saw me, it would be a toss up: they would never speak to me again out of sheer embarrassment, or they would fall down laughing and hurt themselves.

Before our next lesson, my wife and I have a prolonged discussion over the kind of outfit I should wear to class. I draw the line at tights, and show up for the next session in tee-shirt and jeans, a suburban Shavion Glover, ready to stomp.

We are introduced to new steps: flap, ball, change; tick tock; spank step, the Buffalo (as in shuffle off to), the "Irish." We put these steps together with the ones learned last week, and suddenly, I find myself in the middle of a routine. A vision appears in the mirror before us: we are in full costume for a recital at the Staller Center in the spring. I am standing resplendent in top hat and tails, a debonair Fred Astaire surrounded by the lovely ladies in my class, leading first one and then the other across the stage. Suddenly I trip over my feet, and the audience gasps. The fantasy disappears, and I am back in class, stumbling my way through the latest routine.

Later in the week, I visit the school of dance on a Tuesday evening. In one studio, aspiring ballerinas float gracefully across the floor. In the other, Dianne is leading the Advanced Tap Class through their paces. Most of the dancers are young, in their 20's to 30's, and their energy and precision are almost professional. I am inspired by the class, and a bit intimidated.

I don't think I will have to worry about a recital—this year.

The Zen of Golf

Many years ago, I worked as a starter at the local country club. It was a summer job, intended to augment my meager salary as a rookie teacher.

My predecessor had just been named as an assistant principal, so I guess the job of starter was beneath him. At any rate, I was glad he had recommended me for the job.

My responsibilities included getting things organized at the first tee early in the morning, making sure everybody started at the time they had chosen, and patrolling the fairways in an electric cart later in the day, ensuring that the players adhered to the rules. If I wanted to carry a golf club and hit a ball once in awhile, that was all right too.

It sounded like a pretty cushy summer job, managing a gentleman's game at a country club, a place, I thought, of manners and refinement.

I could not have been more wrong.

The first thing I learned was that players did not like to be kept waiting on the first tee, especially the less talented ones. Perhaps it was the embarrassment of trying to hit a drive with everybody standing around, reveling in your clumsiness.

Players jostled for position on the line, even though there was a sign-in sheet. Local politicians threw their proverbial weight around, and intimidation was a palpable force on the first tee.

The second thing I learned was that golfers do not like to be reminded about the rules, no matter how polite you are. Of course, the formula continued: the duffers were the worst offenders to a man, driving their electric carts up on the greens, ignoring divots, and generally tearing up the course. Telling a player that he should speed up his play was an invitation for a lawsuit or a firestorm of verbal abuse.

There is an exercise in Zen Buddhism where he who would seek enlightenment should concentrate his thoughts on a round, white stone. I had thought that there would be a Zen-like, monastic aura on the course, where a group of men and women concentrated with incredible intensity on the progress of a little, white pellet.

What I found was an overwhelming atmosphere of tension and stress, for not only were the golfers competing with each other, but they were competing with themselves, the most dangerous opponent of all.

No wonder they snarled like mad dogs when I asked them to replace their divots.

On the course, the rules of sportsmanship were replaced by the practice of gamesmanship: stepping on the other player's ball, embedding it in the turf, or kicking it under a bush; coughing while an opponent is putting; clearing the throat when someone is about to tee off. The tricks are many and nasty.

The interesting thing about golf is that as engaging as the sport is, nobody seems to be enjoying themselves. I cannot remember the last time I saw a smiling golfer.

I have seen golfers throw their clubs into the water, and wrap an expensive iron around a tree. There's a lot of frustration in this game.

Yet to say that golf is popular is an understatement. In recent years there has been a proliferation of golf courses on Long Island, surpassing potato fields and wineries. At last count, there were more than 250 courses. There are over a million golf sites on the internet, and folks are planning their retirement homes based on accessibility to golf courses.

Wherever there are golfers, there are golf s stories. One of my favorites, which really happened, goes as follows:

A player had a heart attack on the second tee of the local golf course. As the rest of his foursome stood around, waiting for the ambulance to arrive, some other players arrived on the scene. After waiting for a moment, one of them gestured towards the dead man and said, "Do you think he would mind if we played through?"

Another story: It seems a woman had cancer and had to undergo chemotherapy. As a result, she lost her hair, and had to wear a wig and hat when she attended the prestigious Tradition Tournament in Arizona, featuring the likes of Arnold Palmer, Jack Nicklaus, and other stars. As she stood in the gallery, her hat and hairpiece were blown off by a gust of wind and tumbled onto the first tee just as the stars approached. Without a moment's hesitation, the plucky woman walked to the tee, retrieved her hair, and said, "Gentlemen, the wind is blowing from left to right." It is said that the applause could be heard as far away as the 18th hole.

I returned to the golf course a few years later, thinking about such things as golf as a metaphor for life, that we spend our years and a lot of money in pursuit of perfection. I talked to the pro, who told me that nowadays there were two starters and two rangers keeping an eye on things. He said that the course is about to introduce a new computer system that assigns starting times on a five-day, rotating, call-in basis, the ultimate in fairness. He said that in spite of the fact that no one will be able to bribe or pressure the starters, someone is bound to find fault with the new arrangement. He added, "I've learned a lot about human nature on this job."

Note: In June, 2011, after more than 40 years of playing golf, the author got his first hole in one. It was on a 112-yard hole, and he used a hybrid club.

She Opened Her Home to the World: The Life and Times of Betty Puleston

When Betty Puleston met her husband Dennis at a sailing race near Rye, New York, she was in the water, having fallen overboard. Dennis, ever the gentleman, jumped from the officials' boat to save her. He said, "How are you?" She replied, "How are you?"

Betty was impressed with the dashing naval architect and yachtsman who was to sail the South Seas, dine with cannibals, and dally with Samoan maidens, as revealed in his book *Blue Water Vagabond*. When they married in 1939, she thought she might be going on similar jaunts around the world with her husband.

However, that dream was to be put on hold for awhile. There was a war going on, and her husband was developing an amphibious landing craft that would be used in Okinawa and the Normandy Landing.

Betty and her husband, who had taken a job with Brookhaven Laboratory after the war, moved to a compound in the Hamlet of Brookhaven and proceeded to raise a family of four children, born three years apart: Dennis Edward, Jennifer, Pete, and Sally.

While her husband was establishing himself as a naturalist, author, artist, and founding chairman of the Environmental Defense Fund, Betty pursued her own interests. She and Helen Stark started a play school for local children. When some local youngsters were breaking windows in the Brookhaven railroad station, Betty founded the Junior Village Association. Soon she and the youngsters were replacing the broken windows, and went on to plant trees at Squassex Landing. Offering pony rides

131

and puppetry, the Cub Scout leader began to attract youth from the surrounding area.

The Puleston compound became a hub of creative energy, intellectual activity, and social interaction. Betty would take a group of youngsters from the country and introduce them to the city, going to museums and Central Park. Then she would take a group of inner city children and bring them out to the country for pony rides and puppet shows. Betty and Bob Starke held several horse shows, complete with an announcer from Madison Square Garden. During the International Year of the Child, Betty provided space and facilities for the birth of Common Thread, a banner-making project inspired by artist Michael Ince that would spread around the world and end with a presentation at the United Nations. In later years, refugees from Sierra Leone, Croatia, and other countries would be invited to spend time at the Puleston compound.

Along with the refugees from other countries and children from North Bellport and Harlem, another group found their way to Betty's home. Led by George Stoney, whom Betty had met many years before at the Henry Street Settlement House in New York City, there were Milos Forman and Ivan Passer from Czechloslovakia; Colin Lowe, Dalton Muir, and many others from the National Film Board of Canada.

After her children had grown, Betty finally got to travel the world with family friend and filmmaker George Stoney, working on various projects that more often than not had a social context: planned parenthood in India and China, educational reform in Brazil, representing the USIA in Nigeria, Turkey, and Mexico, helping people with special needs in Appalachia.

Recently, Betty and Lynne Jackson produced a film called "Race or Reason: The Bellport Dilemma," which was screened at the Museum of Modern Art in New York, and will be shown locally at the Old South Haven Presbyterian Church on June 8, at 7:00 p.m.

In 1970, there was an outbreak of hostilities between African-American and white students at Bellport High School that forced school officials to call in the police and close school for over a week. Betty opened her home to students and their parents, giving them a place to air their grievances. Video cameras were used to facilitate dialogue. At the time, Betty described the use of video as "a way for people to get to know each other better." In the following weeks, teams of youths interviewed neighbors from the community, which would be played back to residents to other parts of town. Thus a dialogue was established. A meeting was held at a local church, sponsored by the Better Relations Committee for Constructive Action, a group of about thirty high schools students that had grown out of the meetings held at Betty's house.

In 1996, Betty donated the use of land and equipment to the Hamlet Organic Garden, a cooperative farm that has enriched the lives of many local families. She also served as a Chairperson for her alma mater, The City and Country School in New York.

On Tuesday morning, April 28, this generous woman with a great laugh and an amazing hug, this woman who liked to talk to strangers, this woman who opened her home and her heart to the world, took her final trip at the age of 91. At her side was her family, and her life-long friend George, who had taken the last train out of New York that night to be with her at the end.

Betty is predeceased by her husband Dennis, who died in 2001 at the age of 95, and their first-born, archaeologist Dennis Edward, who died when he was struck by lightning on top of El Castillo pyramid at Chichen Itza, Yucatan in 1978. She is survived by two daughters, Jennifer Clement of Brookhaven, and Sally McIntosh, of New Brunswick, Canada, and a son, Pete, also of New Brunswick, seven gifted and talented grandchildren, and seven great grandchildren, who will no doubt make their mark on the world. She is also survived by two sisters, Nancy Lee of Bellport, and Patricia Barron, of S. Dartmouth, Massachusetts.

One of Betty's favorite stories was the Grimm Brothers' tale of the stone soup. In the story, some travelers come to a village during a famine, carrying an empty pot. The villagers are unwilling to share any of their food. The travelers fill the pot with water, and drop a large stone into it and place it over a fire in the village square. One of the villagers asks the travelers what they are doing, and are told they are making stone soup, which would taste better if it had a little garnish and spices. The villagers begin to come forward with ingredients for the soup, and finally a delicious meal is enjoyed by all. The moral: By working together, with everyone contributing what they can, a greater good is achieved. Betty lived by this principle.

A "stone soup" celebration of Betty's life is planned for May 23 at the Puleston compound. Perhaps her life and times may be summed up by the words of a poet, who said, "Let me live in a house by the side of the road and be a friend to man."

Would you like to see your manuscript become a book?

If you are interested in becoming a PublishAmerica author, please submit your manuscript for possible publication to us at:

acquisitions@publishamerica.com

You may also mail in your manuscript to:

PublishAmerica
PO Box 151
Frederick, MD 21705

www.publishamerica.com